ADVANCE PRAISE

"As someone who has built many enterprise software sales teams, I was surprised to discover a fresh and compelling approach to winning the complex sale in *Selling Is Hard. Buying Is Harder.* B2B buyer behaviors are changing, and Garin's buyer enablement methodology makes it easier to buy and accelerates the buying process. Every software sales and presales professional should understand and apply the principles in this book."

—JONATHAN TEMPLE, Operating Partner at The Riverside Company and former CEO at HEAT Software

"Today, more than ever, we live in a world of information overload. Helping buyers make sense of all the information is key to building confidence. What our research shows is that the best go-to-market sales strategies focus more on helping buyers buy and not just helping sellers sell. Garin Hess captures the essence of modern buyer enablement with actionable, evidence-based steps that put the customer's problem, not your product, at the heart of your sales strategy."

—ALASTAIR WOOLCOCK, Gartner Research & Advisory

"With his technology-supported buyer enablement approach, Garin has elegantly flipped the buyer and seller paradigm. The approach not only empowers your customer champion to do the complex internal sale for you, but it also creates more personalized, lasting business solutions. This new approach allows presales people to happily say yes to one of their historically most hated requests—give me your standard demo. Now presales people can deliver their standard demo without investing time and get automated discovery and qualification delivered for free. This will certainly enhance the often troubled relationship between sales and presales."

—KEVIN O'BRIEN, Global VP Presales and Virtual Experience at SAP

"Make it easier for the buyer to buy—and you make it easier for the seller to sell. In this tactical guide to buyer enablement, Garin Hess breaks down this winning equation into actionable steps. Hess shares hard-won insights gleaned from his software startup experience, case studies, and the latest research on what buyers want and need from sellers and how to successfully implement a customer-focused sales effort through automation and personal touch."

—JULIE HANSEN, author of *Sales Presentations for Dummies* and
Act Like a Sales Pro

"At last, here is *the* book on effective B2B selling by the champion of the buyer enablement concept! Garin has been one of the few voices calling out the need to create consensus among the large and growing number of buyers involved in the typical B2B decision. His work becomes more important as companies continue to expand, flatten, and become more virtual. Garin does a masterful job of awakening the B2B selling and marketing community to our true calling as buyer enablers. He has written the guide to the one true way to sell—helping buyers buy."

—WAYNE CERULLO, Founder at B2P Partners

"A major reason why complex sales are lost occurs when salespeople present a solution that does not meet the needs and priorities of behind-the-scenes decision makers. *Selling is Hard. Buying is Harder.* shows you how to get more key stakeholders to engage and reveal their needs during the earlier phases of their buying process. It's a blueprint for creating buyer consensus much faster than your competitors."

—KEVIN DAVIS, author of *The Sales Manager's Guide to Greatness*

"A very successful senior sales colleague said that the best offerings are 'easy to sell, easy to buy.' 'Easy to sell' is all about creating a desirable product. This eye-opening book explores the 'easy to buy' side of the equation, providing compelling insights supported by persuasive data and step-by-step guidelines to enable practical implementation. Garin Hess proposes, presents, and proves a new paradigm for enterprise sales."

—PETER E. COHAN, author of *Great Demo! How to Create and Execute Stunning Software Demonstrations*

"In *Selling Is Hard. Buying Is Harder.,* Garin Hess flips the script on conventional wisdom in business to business (B2B) marketing and sales. Too often, 'customer-focused' teams are anything but. Instead, they focus on *their* process, *their* software, and *their* objectives. It's no surprise most B2B marketing and sales fails to deliver a consistent return on investment. Here's the simple truth: It's not about you. Rather than focus on ourselves, we must learn how to focus on the buyer inside their own company, giving them the tools they need to navigate organizational culture and politics. In his book, Hess will not only convince you that buyer enablement is the key to your success but also provide you the step-by-step action plan to make it happen."

—JASON VOIOVICH, author, speaker, and marketing historian

GARIN HESS

SELLING IS HARD

BUYING

IS HARDER

HOW BUYER ENABLEMENT DRIVES DIGITAL SALES AND SHORTENS THE SALES CYCLE

RIVER GROVE
BOOKS

Published by River Grove Books
Austin, TX
www.rivergrovebooks.com

Distributed by River Grove Books

Design and composition by Greenleaf Book Group and Brian Phillips
Cover design by Greenleaf Book Group and Brian Phillips
Photos on page 112 used by permission of Matthieu Robert-Ortis

Publisher's Cataloging-in-Publication data is available.

Print ISBN: 978-1-63299-294-9

eBook ISBN: 978-1-63299-295-6

First Edition

To Mr. Swallow, my fourth-grade teacher,
who taught all of us to believe everything is possible
if only you make the attempt.

Walk the same road,
Arrive at the same destination.

You're the same you.

Walk a different road,
Arrive at a different destination.

You're a different you.

—Garin Hess

CONTENTS

THE VALUE PROPOSITION OF BUYER ENABLEMENT

The concepts and methodologies for buyer enablement described in this book didn't come all at once. Like most inventions, they started in the seedbed of pain. In 2009, while I was running my last software startup, there was a period where my company was overwhelmed with leads. While that was a good problem to have, my small sales team could not keep up. So I jumped in and started taking sales calls.

One of the first things buyers want is a demo, so I also had to begin doing a lot of demos. One day, I did six demos, back-to-back, and was exhausted. I thought to myself, *I just did the same thing over and over for six hours! There has got to be a better way to do this.* (Well, the demos weren't *exactly* the same; I would ask questions and adjust the demo content in response to the specific interests of the prospects.)

These demos are a bottleneck, I thought. *This is why sales can't keep up.* That realization was the start of a journey that led to my participation in helping to develop the new field of buyer enablement technology for software companies. The results have been astounding so far: Companies that employ buyer enablement technology and principles have seen their close rates jump by more than 40% while simultaneously seeing their sales cycles shorten as much as 62%.

Slow and Frustrating: Life Before Buyer Enablement

When working with the sales team for my previous startup, I did some investigation and discovered that, on average, our reps had to deliver about four to five demos to close a deal. There were the demos for new leads exploring our product for the first time and demos for each additional stakeholder brought into the purchasing decision. Our analysis also showed we did one to three demos for deals that either stalled or were later lost to a competitor.

I recognized the potential of a vicious cycle: The more leads we brought into the pipeline, the more demos we had to do, which increased the demand on an already overtaxed staff. That is, getting better at the top of the marketing funnel created an exponential scaling problem later, no matter how many salespeople or supporting product specialists we hired. What were our options?

Problem 1: Scaling Our Demo Capability

Since high demand for demos was a core issue, I began to wonder, *Who should we be doing demos for?* We obviously could not do them for every single person who asked for one; nobody has that kind of capacity. So we began trying to qualify leads better and telling less qualified leads that we could not do a live demo for them. But that seemed like a terrible trade-off. Which raised the next question: Was it necessary to tell some of our leads that we simply could not provide a demo, or could we automate the process in some way?

We began experimenting. We put product videos on YouTube. We recorded webinars and sent out links. We got feedback that those efforts were only partially helpful. Prospects said it was too difficult to find exactly what they were looking for, and the information they did find was not personalized, so many quickly lost interest. The lack of personalization meant that the prospects were reluctant to pass what we sent them on to others. As one stakeholder told us, "I can't just send this 45-minute WebEx recording to my CEO. He'll never watch it. I'd like to bring him in on a live demo. When can we schedule that?"

In terms of reducing our workload, this experiment was a complete failure. "Success" just increased the demand for live demos, which compounded our original problem.

Beyond scaling issues, I began thinking about the impact this would have on sales cycles as well. If we have to demo four to five times to close a deal, and it takes two to three weeks on average to schedule an appointment with every new stakeholder inside the target organization, that's eight to fifteen weeks at a minimum we've added to our sales cycle.

Problem 2: Time Is the Thief of Closes

As every experienced sales rep knows, the longer it takes for a customer to reach a decision, the harder it is to close the sale. The more the process drags on, the more likely it is that problems will appear:

- A key decision maker may be promoted or leave the company, which means the buying team needs to regroup.
- Other priorities can take over the stakeholders' attention.
- Infighting can occur because the team never got aligned around problems or solutions early on.
- As stakeholders trickle in and out of the process, decisions you thought were final get revisited. The understanding of buying criteria shifts day to day.

In my case, the issue of long sales cycles became most evident when we started getting into a lot of conversations with large customers that had complex information technology (IT) security requirements. They would send us a spreadsheet about our security and data protection policies with more than 200 questions to fill out (still a common practice), then we would have to have a discussion with the IT department and finally participate in a post-discussion question and answer period before we could be approved.

This started coming up over and over. There was a pattern. We would get to a certain point in the sales process, and predictably the prospect would say, "The IT department needs to give approval." While it was a strong buying signal, I began dreading that step. The whole process of meeting the needs of a new stakeholder group could easily add two to four weeks to the sales cycle and take an additional eight to ten hours of our time for every deal. Again, another bottleneck. Again, we started experimenting.

As we looked at the pattern of questions that IT departments wanted, my team decided to put together our own set of questions, answers, and policy documents that should satisfy most IT departments. Instead of waiting for the moment when the IT department wanted to get involved, we became *proactive*, telling them what needed to happen. Early in their interactions with prospects, our reps would say something like, "It's likely your IT department will want to get involved. Would you please find the right contact there and tell them you're interested in purchasing and then give them these documents?"

Amazingly, this cut our need to engage with the IT departments more than 60%. And when we did engage, it was a shorter conversation where we needed to answer fewer questions (because the most common questions had been answered by the documents we gave them).

That was eye-opening: When we knew exactly what they were going to want and supplied it before they even asked for it, everything went faster. We could do in days or weeks what normally stretched out over months in traditional selling.

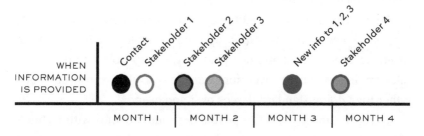

PROVIDING INFO IN TRADITIONAL SELLING

THE BUYER ENABLEMENT APPROACH

Figure 1: Taking Control of Information: Being able to anticipate buyer information needs and having the right materials prepared drastically cut the time it took Consensus to reach critical buyers.

What we had stumbled upon was a buyer enablement mentality, and our staff became dedicated to a simple goal: What can we do to make it easier for the people promoting us inside an account to sell for us?

Enter Buyer Enablement Technology

While my previous company had largely solved the issue of meeting the needs of various IT stakeholders, we never did solve the demo bottleneck problem. I became determined to find a solution. Demos are an essential part of every purchasing decision, and I began to think, *What if we applied the same thinking that we did with the IT department to demos? What if we anticipate what the prospects are going to want and send it to them before they realize they want it?*

A few years later, I started the company I run now: Consensus™. One of my key drivers was to design the technology to automate the repetitive aspects of demoing. That way, salespeople and especially sales engineers can be saved for strategic consultative conversations rather than doing standard demos over and over.

To replace these repetitive people-dependent demos with technology, we needed to understand what made live demos so important in sales:

- First, because a sales rep is there in person, they can tailor the information so the prospect gets the demo that they want—one that addresses their specific questions and concerns.

- Second, the salesperson can ask questions to discover more about the prospect's interests and needs.

- Third, in the process of conversation, the rep can get leads to additional stakeholders who need to get involved to get the deal done.

Could we do this with technology? The answer was yes. We created software that would allow potential buyers to customize their experience with a demo and share links with others in their organization. We spent some time developing content targeted at different stakeholders and then did a launch.

We were immediately blown away as soon as we began to test it with our own sales team. The second day, one target company began sharing the demo around their organization like crazy. Within two hours, 12 people had watched our demo. Within three weeks, they purchased. Because of the number of stakeholders involved, I knew from experience this same deal would have normally taken months to close. This was a completely different way to sell.

Not long after, we began seeing others in the software industry who were using the same approach have success as well. While employing buyer enablement concepts and supporting technology at a large IT software firm, where he was the global head of inside sales, a mentor and friend of mine and business-to-business (B2B) sales guru texted me: "We just closed a $70,000 deal in twelve days, a process that normally takes six to nine months."

TRADITIONAL SELLING

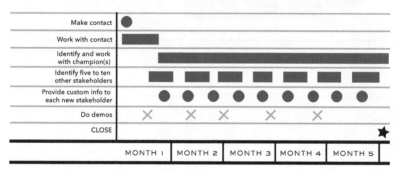

TECHNOLOGY-ENABLED
BUYER ENABLEMENT SELLING

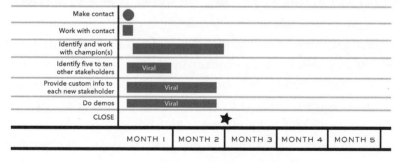

Figure 2: A Completely Different Way to Sell: Using all the tools of buyer enablement allows buyers to reach purchasing decisions much quicker than in traditional selling. Buying cycles can drop anywhere from 40%–60%.

Later that year, we had a customer come to us and say, "We've been measuring the impact of your automated demo software on our close rate and sales cycle, and both have improved." We asked them for the results: Sales cycle was cut by more than half; close rates improved by more than 40%.

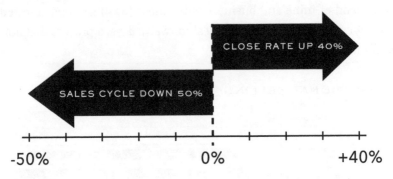

CLOSE RATE UP 40%

SALES CYCLE DOWN 50%

-50%   0%   +40%

Figure 3: ROI of Buyer Enablement: A Consensus customer reported their sales cycle dropped at least by half and their close rates rose 40% once they started using buyer enablement strategies and technologies.

Buyer Enablement and Digital Sales Transformation

One assumption we made when designing our intelligent demo automation software is that the nature of selling is changing, not because how to sell has fundamentally changed but because of two driving forces: Buying behaviors are changing, and going digital with sales content (such as interactive video demos) opens up new ways of approaching old problems.

Buyers today want to learn at their own pace, and they want to learn when and where they are ready, not when you are ready. They want access and they want it now. This buying behavior change has driven organizations to provide more self-directed digital access to key information in the sales process, often called *digital selling*.

Many organizations are partway through a digital sales transformation initiative. The most important question in any digital selling program is not "How do we make our sales process digital?" but "How should going digital change the way we sell?" and "What opportunities does going digital open up that we didn't have before?" In other words, going digital opens up new ways to approach sales more effectively.

And if we flip the script, the question becomes "How does going digital change the way buyers buy?"

As an example, we were surprised to find out how much more effective a first appointment could be if we could get the prospect to engage with digital content in the gap between the time the first appointment was set and the time it was held. Instead of waiting for the appointment and losing that time and momentum, now the gap between appointments becomes an opportunity to use digital assets to drive further engagement, discover stakeholders, and shorten the buying process.

We began asking ourselves, what kind of content does the buyer need at each stage to make progress? How can we get them to engage with that content in between appointments and share that with other stakeholders? By answering these questions, we discovered that not only providing this kind of digital access "in the gaps" but also recommending and encouraging it is yet another way to make buying easier.

Buyer Enablement: What's Not to Love?

When writing this book, I relied largely on my own experience and observation in B2B sales and in talking with other B2B sales leaders and professionals. I held more than 40 interviews with sales leaders from all over the world, mostly in the technology industry. In my online research, what I found was bits and pieces of disconnected but relevant information from sources like Gartner and CEO Insights that, in my opinion, backed up my own experiences.

I found studies showing that it's important to understand how customers buy, studies about the need to provide personalized content to buyers, and surveys showing the ineffectiveness of most demos. But I didn't find any sources that explored how all these issues are connected nor showed how technology can overcome the challenges and make buyer enablement scalable and a reality that can be a game changer.

Pulling together all those disconnected strings is one of the main purposes of this book. Buyer enablement is a practice that can benefit any business, and many of the principles discussed in this book apply to any sector. I've been involved in technology sales for over 20 years now, so that environment provides the context for all the examples in this book.

My own personal experience struggling with improving how we sold software illustrates the return on investment (ROI) of moving toward technology-supported buyer enablement:

- Making it easier for champions to do the selling for you
- Reaping the rewards of shorter sales cycles and higher close rates

Let me be clear. You will see great results employing the concepts in this book with or without technology. However, when you combine the concepts and framework with technology that supports buyer enablement, the benefits are multiplied. When buyer enablement becomes the driving force behind your digital selling approach, you'll see the most dramatic decrease in the length of sales cycle you've ever experienced.

The key to getting these results is understanding what your buyers need before they know they need it and giving it to them in such a way that every stakeholder can get what they need as quickly as possible. By anticipating and giving the buyers what they need before they even realize they need it, you will help them naturally get to a decision faster (which equals a shorter sales cycle). And because each interested stakeholder gets what they need, they tend to come to alignment more often (which results in higher closing rates). In other words, they get to consensus faster.

Again, I want to emphasize that buyer enablement relies on more than just technology. In fact, I realized early on that the technology alone wasn't enough. It had to be coupled with a new mentality among our reps about when and how to engage different stakeholders. Their expertise in leveraging the technology to provide each buyer with the right information at the right time was what led to shorter sales cycles and higher close rates. These insights are what eventually led to the principles and methodology in this book.

ACKNOWLEDGMENTS

Most of the individuals and organizations who contributed to the content of this book are already mentioned in the footnotes. While the concepts and framework I advocate arise from my experience, their supporting ideas, research, and comments bolster and strengthen, resulting in a more persuasive argument.

Thanks to Rex Galbraith for coming up with the term *DEEP-C* for my buyer enablement framework and John Cook and Jon Temple for coining the title. They are some of the best sales and marketing professionals and business leaders I've ever worked with. Thank you to Sue Reynard and Lindsey Clark, my editors, and to the project team at River Grove Books for helping to bring the final product to a higher standard.

And last of all, thank you to my wife, Kristin, who cheerfully accompanied me on several book-writing trips when I needed to hunker down to complete the writing. She has always supported me and cheered me on, and that has always meant the world to me.

TAKING CHARGE OF BUYING

"Intelligence is the ability to adapt to change."
—UNKNOWN

When does your success become risky? When you are unwilling to change. And buying behaviors are definitely changing, which means sales behaviors need to change as well.

Sales enablement and its associated technologies have grown rapidly in recent years. Their underlying premise is sound: providing sales reps with easy access to the specific information and resources they need to execute their sales process. Sounds great, right?

It is—at least to a point. Sales enablement technologies have had a major positive impact on the ability of salespeople to follow and apply standard selling methods to their organizations. There is a problem, however. When it comes to sales effectiveness, study after study shows that the real challenge for salespeople is to get better at understanding and facilitating their customers' buying process.

In short, B2B sales isn't really about what sellers are doing; it's about what our buyers are doing. Interactions between your champions—the people promoting you inside an account—and their coworkers are where either the magic happens or a deal tanks. And right now, it's a lot more of the latter. How do we turn this trend around?

While you've probably already purchased some tech to support sales enablement, that tech is, at best, only *half of the equation* (if that). It makes salespeople more efficient, which is great, but it doesn't do much to enable the other half of the sale: the group of people making the buying decision.

Take Charge of Buying; Let Go of Selling

Suppose you're on a journey through the Amazon, and your guide turns to you and says, "Well, here we are at a fork in the river. What do you think we ought to do next?"

Wouldn't you be thinking to yourself, *Well, that's what I paid you to know?*

Most likely, you'd rather the guide say something like this: "Okay, we're at a fork in the river. If we go left, here's where it will take us. If we go right, we'll arrive at this other location. This is what I recommend we do right now, and here is why."

Effectively, that is what we need to do as sales professionals. Adopting a guide mentality is key to buyer enablement. And to do that, you need to rethink what might be some long-held assumptions. Let me ask you two questions with seemingly obvious answers about B2B sales:

- Who is in charge of selling?
- Who is in charge of buying?

Most would answer that the B2B sales team is in charge of selling, and the prospect and any accompanying influencers and decision makers (aka the buying group) are in charge of buying.

Will you be surprised if I tell you it is just the opposite?

It's true: The B2B sales team is in charge of buying, and the buyer is in charge of selling.

"Okay, Mr. Wise Guy," you say. "Stop talking in circuitous riddles and get to your point."

Let's look at selling first.

You Are Not in Charge of Selling–the Buyer Is

In buyer enablement, you are shifting your mindset from selling to enabling the buyer(s). Instead of the focus being on you, the focus is on them. What this means is that, yes, you need to sell to (educate, consult, persuade, etc.) the champion, but after that, you need to empower and equip the champion to sell for you. While you can help, the internal champion is the one who is going to go get the deal done.

So who is doing the selling? You or the buyer? The buyer. That initial buyer—the one who has decided that your solution is best for them and their company—has to sell to the rest of the buying group. It's unavoidable.

"I know the person I'm dealing with is going to have to pitch internally. In large organizations, the CFO is not going to get on the phone with me," said Kristin Nagel, senior account manager for ZoomInfo.

In truth, you'll both be selling to the buying group, but largely the buying group is going to look to the internal change agent, or champion (referred to as the "mobilizer" in *The Challenger Sale*[1]), to lead them through the process of making a purchase decision. You are just an enabler.

---

1 Matthew Dixon and Brent Adamson, *The Challenger Sale: Taking Control of the Customer Conversation* (New York City: Penguin, 2011).

The Buyer Is Not in Charge of Buying–You Are

How many times has your buyer gone through the purchasing process for the product or solution you are selling? Usually never! As an example, if they are purchasing a customer relations management (CRM) system, how many times have they purchased this system? In their career, this is likely the only time they've done it.

Paul Norris, a veteran solution-consulting leader and former vice president at CA Technologies, told me, "People that buy software aren't good at it. They don't do it often. Internally, the process is not understood."[2]

On the other hand, how many times have you experienced the buying process that goes along with purchasing your product or solution? It's probably too many to count. Depending on your product and industry and how long you've been in your role, perhaps hundreds of times. Even if you're a newbie, you're still on a team, and collectively as a team, you have deep expertise among you about the buying process and potential pitfalls on the journey. Whatever the case, you've been through it many more times than the buyer. And because you have so much more experience in the buying process, who needs to take charge and lead the buyer through the buying process? You do.

Too many sales reps ask the buyer, "What do you think are the next steps?" I'm not saying this is a completely irrelevant question or shouldn't sometimes be part of the process, but generally speaking, buyers want and need you to exert leadership, to be their guide. Even if they don't realize it for themselves, they need you to take the lead. They don't know what they should be doing. They don't know the questions to ask, the relevant pros and cons to consider, or the different roles of stakeholders they need to involve to get the deal done and change implemented in their organizations.

As an example, how many times have you encountered a buyer who says something like, "I think we have everyone we need involved,"

---

2   Paul Norris, in discussion with the author, January 26, 2018.

only to find out later that there are others who need to be a part of the process. That's not their mistake; it's yours. You should know that the kind of product you're selling and the kind of company you're selling to usually requires input and decision-making from specific roles inside this kind of organization. *You* are in charge of the buying process, not the buyer. Take the lead. Show them the way. They will appreciate it, and you'll get deals done faster.

Buyer enablement means making buying easier by taking charge of the buying process in order to help your customer sell for you.

Make Buying Easier

Buyer enablement isn't as much about convincing buyers that they have a need that should be solved as it is about helping to make the buying process easier. The easier you make the process for the buyer, the sooner they will take the actions necessary to move through the purchasing process and the faster they will make a decision. Moreover, if you can make the process easier on them, they are more likely to choose you as a vendor (a nice side benefit, wouldn't you say?). But how do you make the buying process easier?

As with sales enablement, buyer enablement is providing people with easy access to tools and information they need to keep a purchase moving forward, only here the "people" are the buyers inside your target organizations, not your salespeople.

There are traditional, low-tech ways to support these buyers as they sell for you internally in their companies, but the real leading edge is to use technology to customize the buying experience to each decision maker at each step of the process.

The buyer enablement approach shifts the responsibility of getting the deal done from your shoulders to the shoulders of your champion and the buying group. In reality, *you* can't get the deal done anyway—only the buyers can sign the contract. So you need to change your mindset from "What do I need to do to get this deal done?" to "What does my champion and the buying group need to do to get this purchase done?"

> When buyer enablement combines prescriptive advice and practical support at multiple points across jobs, it becomes a powerful tool for sales to drive customers to buy their solutions. Not only does information help customers perceive a job as easier, but information also helps customers successfully buy a solution, reducing later regret. **–GARTNER**[3]

Buyer Enablement as a Competitive Advantage

Making buying easier is the essence of buyer enablement, but it isn't just about closing that next deal. It's also about an approach to your market that will set you apart from your competition. Companies who are easy to buy from have a huge competitive advantage. "77% of buyers agree that purchases have become very complex and difficult."[4]

To gain this competitive advantage, you and your teams need to understand what buyers want and how they think; you need to discover and engage the buying group; you need to equip the champion to sell for you to that buying group; and you need to prescriptively guide your champion through the buying process. You're their guide on what otherwise would likely be a disastrous journey.

Become a master of buyer enablement and you will shorten your sales cycle and close more deals at the same time.

---

3   Gartner, *Win More B2B Sales Deals*, Brent Adamson, 2018.
4   Gartner, *Win More B2B Sales Deals*.

PART I

CUSTOMER FOCUS AND BUYER EMPATHY: LEAVE YOUR WORLD BEHIND AND GET BETTER RESULTS

CHAPTER 1

DEVELOPING BUYER EMPATHY

"Empathy is one of our greatest tools of business that is most underused."

—DANIEL LUBETZKY[1]

In Celeste Headlee's now famous TED Talk, "10 Ways to Have a Better Conversation," she says, "Most of us don't listen with the intent to understand. We listen with the intent to reply."[2]

Doesn't this epitomize an ineffective salesperson or sales engineer? How many demos have you attended (as a buyer) where the solution consultant wasn't consulting at all but rather going through the same demo they do over and over, almost entirely disregarding your specific interests or needs? How many sales conversations have you had (as a buyer) where you didn't feel listened to?

As sales professionals, we've all fallen into this trap ourselves from time to time. We think more about ourselves than our customer. That mentality has to change if we are to become more customer focused, which is a prerequisite for successfully enacting buyer enablement.

---

1   Carolyn Sun, "5 Business Lessons from KIND Founder and CEO Daniel Lubetzky," Entrepreneur, October 7, 2015, https://www.entrepreneur.com/article/251438.

2   Celeste Headlee, "10 Ways to Have a Better Conversation," TEDxCreativeCoast, May 2015, https://www.ted.com/talks/celeste_headlee_10_ways_to_have_a_better_conversation.

It's Not About Us

If we peel back the layers of ineffectiveness in B2B sales, we'll almost always see one principle at the root of this problem: As sellers, we are too self-centered.

We are, as Ms. Headlee describes, "listening with the intent to reply" rather than to understand. What are we thinking about while we're supposed to be listening? We are thinking about how we're behind on our numbers, about the next conversation two hours from now with a higher-profile prospect, about what our next move is, about how we can handle that objection the client is bringing up, or about any number of things that could help us close the deal.

What we aren't thinking about is *them*—the buyer—and what they are thinking and feeling. About *their* journey. About what they are risking to even consider our solution. We unwittingly think that selling is about what we do rather than what the buyer does. And the irony is that selling isn't about us; it's about them—you need to understand your buyer more deeply.

The Power of Buyer Empathy

In Jennifer Lynn Barnes's book *Killer Instinct*, a law enforcement profiler remarks, "Maybe, to do what you and I do, we have to have a little bit of the monster in us."[3] This profiler wants to anticipate the next move of the criminal by understanding how they think. They do that by putting themselves in the shoes of someone else, by trying to look at the world the same way that person does. That is empathy. And for a profiler, the "someone else" is the criminal.

When you practice this skill at the workplace, it becomes business empathy, which can be a valuable asset. Great business leaders have the ability to intuitively imagine the thoughts and feelings of their employees. It helps them make better decisions. Great employees

3   Jennifer Lynn Barnes, *Killer Instinct* (White Plains, New York: Disney-Hyperion, 2015).

have the ability to imagine the thoughts and feelings of their leaders, helping them deliver better collaboration and results.

To become better at selling, you have to pursue a particular type of business empathy that I call buyer empathy. That means understanding how buyers view the world: what they think, what they want, how they behave, what influences their decisions. Buyers aren't criminals, of course (except when they talk you down to a 40% discount), but what I'm suggesting is that as sellers, do what profilers do and tap into "the buyer in us." Doing so can help us anticipate what they need, what their next move will be.

In other words, to know what you need to do, you need to first understand how buyers think, what they want, and how they behave. Then you'll know exactly how to enable them and close more sales.

A Buyer's View of the Universe

There are a lot of things that buyers think about. By and large, you, the seller, are not one of them (see Figure 4). Take a minute to think about what that means to you as a salesperson. To be successful, every time you make contact with a prospect, you need to be offering them something that helps *them* be successful in one or more of these spheres that concern them.

THE PROSPECT'S UNIVERSE

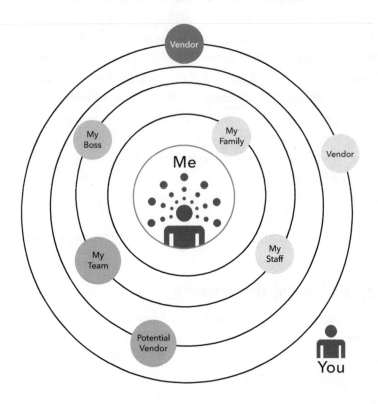

© 2018 Gartner, Inc.

Figure 4: To me, this Gartner graphic is representative of "How Buyers See the Universe": You, the seller, are barely on the radar of a buyer initially. You have to raise their awareness and their recognition that making a change to your solution can improve their universe.

As Gartner puts it, "Think of your audience as the center of a universe that you need to navigate. If you talk too much about yourself and your products, prospects will disengage almost immediately since that information is not relevant to them."[4]

The first step on the journey to buyer enablement is to keep the prospect's universe in your head.

---

4   Gartner, *Tech Go-to-Market: The Ideal First Sales Meeting Agenda and Presentation*, Michele Buckley, January 30, 2018.

"Sales teams have to bring more insights and become buyer-centric, not product-centric. They have to be able to contextualize the products and solutions into prospects' industry, unique challenges, and even into their organization." —KEVIN JOYCE, CMO AND VP OF STRATEGY SERVICES AT THE PEDOWITZ GROUP[5]

Remember Buyers Are People

This may sound simplistic, but too often we think of buyers as being limited to their role as prospects, leads, champions, or future customers instead of thinking about them as people—people like you and me. When we dehumanize buyers into just their roles, we won't connect on that emotional level that buyers need from us in order to feel confident.

Part of what tempts us to dehumanize buyers is that we're intimidated by them. We know they hold the keys to something we want, and this influences our thinking. Instead of feeling intimidated, place the focus of your effort on reaching them on a personal level. It doesn't have to be complicated. Even a small connection goes a long way, but it has to be real, not contrived.

Years ago, I heard Robert Harris, the founder of Chem-Dry, an international leader in carpet cleaning franchises, explain the principle that "people are just people" by sharing an extreme example of how he won over some key distributors from Japan. At the time, Chem-Dry was courting a large Japanese distributor and wanted to do a multimillion-dollar deal. To Chem-Dry it was a very big deal, but from the distributor's perspective, Chem-Dry was still an unproven small company. The Japanese delegation had come to visit Harris in California, and after a couple of days of meetings, he took them to his personal mountain retreat. Harris was trying to get a verbal commitment from them, but they were balking and delaying.

---

5   2018 Demand Generation Benchmark Survey Report, https://www.demandgenreport .com/resources/reports/2018-demand-generation-benchmark-survey-report.

Harris was an aviation enthusiast and a stunt pilot. He could see they were at an impasse, so he decided to take a break and invite them to ride with him in his private plane. He took them up, and partway through the ride, he did a full loop. His guests all gasped and then laughed. They were nervous but clearly delighted. Harris laughed with them. Laughing, he asked, "Do we have a deal?" No response.

Taking the laughter as a sign that walls were starting to crumble, Harris decided to push the envelope. He put the plane through a barrel roll. Again, more gasping and laughing. Harris laughed again and asked, "So do we have a deal now?" They laughed back, but still no response. Harris pulled the plane straight up until it stalled, the engine going silent. The plane began to streak downward. Moments later, he roared the engine back to life. Laughs of relief and delight came again. "Do we have a deal yet?" Harris asked again. Finally the answer came back as the delegation leader, laughing, said, "Yes, yes, just take us back down to earth!"

Harris found a way to bring laughter, something that connects all of us, into the conversation, immediately bringing down the walls. Few of us could pull this kind of stunt (pun intended) to get a deal done, but Harris's main point was this: Forget about who you are talking to, forget about how important the deal is to you, and remember that people are people. Don't be intimidated. Treat them like human beings and make a real connection. Good things follow.

YOU NEED TO *ACTUALLY* CARE

There is lots of advice out there about how to relate to people, how to ask open-ended questions, how to show people you are listening, and how to make people feel cared about. In my opinion, most of this advice is useless because it's just a put-on and people see right through it. There is no substitute for actually seeing other people as real people and caring about them. If you do, all else will come naturally.

There Is No Such Thing as a Complex Sale

I've heard many sales reps and leaders describe their task as "complex selling." But I say, "There is no such thing as a 'complex sale.'"

"What?! Blasphemy!" you cry. "I've been through lots of complex sales so believe me, I know."

I'll say it again: There is *no such thing* as a complex sale.

There is only a complex purchase. I'll say it one more time: There are no complex *sales*, only complex *purchases*.

It's not about you. It's about them. Thinking that we, as salespeople, can accelerate sales by changing only what *we* are doing is the height of self-centered sales thinking. We have to get into the minds of the buyers.

A couple of years ago, I backpacked up the highest mountain in the state of Utah in the United States, Kings Peak, with my son's Venture Scout team. It was awe-inspiring to stand in a range of towering mountains at the summit of the tallest and see that there was nothing higher than we were as far as we could see in any direction.

Our group was led by Ben Booth, an experienced outdoorsman and avid fly fisherman. One day, he was explaining to me what he loves about fly-fishing: "You have to get into the mind of the fish," he told me. "Where do they want to be? What do they want to eat? What excites them? What bores them?" On that trip, I saw him repeatedly catch fish in a spot where others weren't catching anything. Why? Because he was in the "mind of the buyer," so to speak (or "mind of the biter," if you like dad-joke-level puns).

The same thinking can be applied to B2B sales. If you think about any transaction as a sale, you tend to focus on what the seller has to do. If you think about it as a purchase, you focus on what the buyer has to do. There is a *big* difference in how you approach the whole process.

The reality is that making a purchase, even an entry-level purchase, has become increasingly difficult and complex. How complex is the complex purchase? Figure 5 says it all:

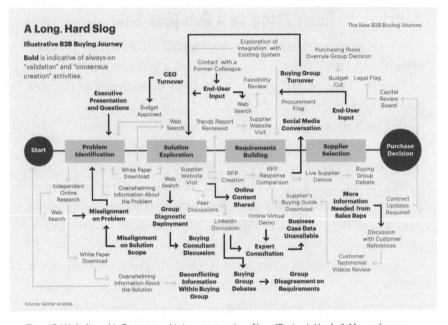

Figure 5: We believe this Gartner graphic is representative of how "Buying Is Harder": Many sales reps still have a simplistic view of the buyer's process in their head. The painful reality of today's purchasing decisions is reflected in this graphic. (Source: Gartner, *Win More B2B Sales Deals*, Brent Adamson, 2018.)

According to Gartner, "The hardest part of B2B solutions isn't selling them, but buying them. Today's buying journey has effectively reached a tipping point where it's become nearly unnavigable without a significant amount of help."[6] Moreover, the buying journey is nonlinear, with complex tasks looping back on each other as different stakeholders get involved.

"All of this looping around and bouncing from one job to another means that buyers value suppliers that make it easier for them to navigate the purchase process. Additionally, purchase ease has a

---

6   Gartner, *Win More B2B Sales Deals,* Brent Adamson, 2018.

significant impact on the value customers perceive from their purchases—and the level of regret they might experience. High levels of regret dramatically reduce customer loyalty and sharply cut the chances a customer will advocate for that supplier."[7]

Are You a Deal Closer? Nope.

There is a t-shirt someone used to wear around our office that proclaimed, "I CLOSE DEALS."

I CLOSE DEALS

Figure 6.

---

7   Gartner, *Win More B2B Sales Deals*, Brent Adamson, 2018.

The problem is, salespeople don't close deals. *What? More blasphemy!* Really, though, who has the power to get a deal done? Only the buyer does. They are the only ones who can ink the deal. You may pat yourself on the back because you've helped them close a lot of deals, and kudos to you if you have, but let's not deceive ourselves by saying, "I close deals." You have helped *them* close the deals. That t-shirt should have said, "My buyers close deals."

Figure 7.

Embracing this mentality isn't as easy as it might sound. To truly achieve our potential in B2B sales, we must rise above ourselves. We have been misguided to think that the best way to achieve our potential and dreams is by focusing on those dreams. Ironically, it's just the opposite. Achieving our potential comes only when the needs of others loom larger than our own needs. Our needs and dreams are met as a by-product.

In a recent article about enterprise sales by Amy Volas, she explains, "It's about putting your customer's need for a solution above your need to make a sale."[8] We must appeal to our best altruistic virtues to change our self-centered mindset. "Virtue is chok'd with foul ambition," Shakespeare observed. By setting our own ambitions to the side and focusing on the buyer and what they need, we'll be able to take the risks needed in order to serve the client best. That, in turn (while it feels risky), actually creates the path most likely to deliver what we want as well.

8   Amy Volas, "The Enterprise Sales Process I've Used to Close $100,000,000+," OpenView Venture Partners, blog, July 25, 2018, https://openviewpartners.com/blog /enterprise-sales-process/#.XV6rl5NKhQL.

CHAPTER 2

HOW BUYERS THINK

"None of us is as dumb as all of us."
—CAPTAIN MARK KELLY

It's no surprise that buyers may see things differently than you do. There wouldn't be anything to negotiate if those on both sides of the table saw everything the same way. To explore this idea more specifically, think about the last sale you lost. Did you lose the deal because the price was too high? Was it the lack of differentiation from competitors? Was your sales presentation poor? What was it exactly? Do you think this reason aligns with your prospect's reasons for not choosing you? It seems to me that the following Gartner graphic shows the stark difference between why buyers disqualify vendors and what vendors *think* is driving their disqualification (Figure 8).

Vendor and Buyer Assessment: What Disqualifies Providers from Consideration

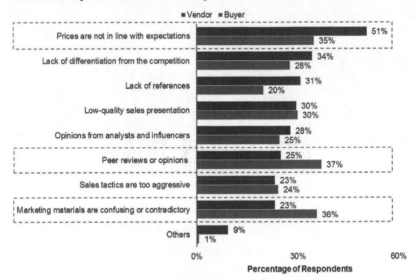

Vendor: Q. What are the top-three reasons why a prospect might disqualify your organization from consideration?
Number of respondents = 172. Up to three ranked responses were permitted.
Buyer: Q. What would cause you to immediately disqualify a [technology] provider from consideration during a buying cycle?
Number of respondents = 508. Up to three responses were permitted, without ranking.
ID: 369858   © 2018 Gartner, Inc.

Figure 8: This Gartner graphic shows the difference between buyer and vendor perception: This chart shows the difference between the factors that vendors (like us) think have cost a sale vs. what buyers say made the difference to them. Prices are not in line with expectations, for example, was cited by 51% of vendors but only 35% of buyers as being a reason why a technology provider would be disqualified from consideration during a buying cycle. (Source: Gartner, *Vendor and Buyer Assessment of Reasons Why Enterprises Disqualify Providers From Consideration*, August 2018.)

For example, vendors consider "prices are not in line with expectations" to be the reason its organization is disqualified 51% of the time, while buyers consider it to be a reason to disqualify a technology provider only 35% of the time.[1] In contrast, this graphic shows that buyers put a much higher priority on peer reviews or opinions than vendors expect.

---

1   Gartner, *Tech Go-to-Market: 3 Disconnects Between Providers and Enterprise Customers That Delay Buying Decisions*, Hank Barnes, August 27, 2018.

To me, the data in Figure 8 is a reminder that many salespeople have misconceptions when it comes to what buyers think about. More specifically, it should change your behavior as a vendor. For example, I believe this research suggests that vendors need to focus more on bolstering value and reducing risk with peer reviews than on providing discounts as a reason to purchase. Let's explore in more detail what issues influence a buyer's thinking and mindset.

Emotional ROI

A traditional way to look at what buyers want is what I call the five P's:

1. Profit ("Think of what I can buy with the money I'll make.")

2. Prestige ("When everyone applauds my promotion at the awards event, I'll know I've achieved a milestone.")

3. Pleasure ("This will make my life easier.")

4. Preservation ("I'm definitely going to keep my job secure with this.")

5. Pain relief ("The #*$&@ user interface is so frustrating; with this new UI, our whole team will love using the CRM again.")

What's interesting is that when most of us try to explain a logical, rational ROI to the customer, it is often at the bottom of their list of their real reasons to buy. Of course, what you're selling has to meet their budget requirements, and they have to believe it will help them move toward their business goals more effectively in one way or another.

What they care most about, however, is what I call the Emotional return on investment, or Emotional ROI. Offering Emotional ROI means that whatever emotional benefits your buyers are going to get out of the purchase will eventually outweigh the emotional risks present when making the purchase in the first place.

What emotional risks are at play in B2B buying? Here are just a few:

Predictability and stability

Prospects put their sense of peace and stability at risk every time they consider implementing a new solution or product. The pain we know is often easier to live with than the unknown. Even if a buyer's future looks less than ideal with their current solution (or lack thereof), at least they're used to the situation and have learned to survive. We may be able to offer them something better, but inevitably there is unpredictability and instability that come along with new solutions.

Peer reputation

When a prospect endorses and promotes a particular solution to their peers, they are putting their reputation on the line. If the purchase and implementation go well and business results follow, their reputation grows immensely. Conversely, if the buying or implementation process is rocky or the solution fails to produce the desired results, the prospect runs the risk of losing the confidence of their peers.

This carries over into relationships with leadership as well. If peer reputation takes a hit when a purchase goes awry, it's possible that your buyer's reputation with their manager will take an even bigger hit. They may be hoping for a promotion, which could be put at risk because they are considering your solution. In short, they may be risking a hit to their definition of success.

Workload and current projects

By adding yet another project to their plate, buyers are putting other projects they already have in progress at risk. If the purchasing process and implementation take too much time, they may not be able to execute effectively on other parts of their job, adding stress and other negative consequences.

Work-life balance

Our relationships, hobbies, and other interests have a dramatic impact on our happiness. Your prospects may be thinking that the 40 hours they'll need to spend implementing your solution will mean 10 less hours with their kids at home or with some other relationship. This is a balance that many buyers aren't willing to trade in exchange for attempting to realize the promised benefits of your solution.

For your prospect to believe in the Emotional ROI of your solution, they need to believe that their reputation will grow, that it will make them more upwardly mobile, that it won't put current projects at risk, and that it will, at the very least, not hurt their outside relationships or interests. Whether it is the Emotional ROI or the personal connection, they will ultimately make the purchase decision based on emotional factors.

Buyers Are Placing More Value on Research

If you were to guess, how long would you say your sales cycle is? I've heard most vendors say four to six months. But Gartner research shows that "resolving all concerns and objections to move forward with a solution (or abandon the buying process entirely) is likely to take buyers 2.6 months. Technology buyers spend on average 16.3 months to complete a new IT purchase."[2] That's more than a ten-month difference. Or put another way, we see that there is a 172% gap between how the vendor thinks of the sales cycle and the reality of the purchasing cycle.

Why the immense gap between what vendors think of as the sales cycle and how long it actually takes? Because buyers are doing so much more research on their own that too often vendors don't qualify for the opportunity until the buyer is deep into their purchasing process. It begs the question—how many buying groups disqualify you as a vendor before you even get to engage with them at all?

---

2   Gartner, *Tech Go-to-Market: Why Tech Sales Cycles Are Taking So Long and What Needs to Be Done Now*, Michele Buckley, June 4, 2018.

The increased reliance on research is understandable. Most B2B buyers have been through a purchasing cycle that didn't work out for them, so they are increasingly likely to spend a lot of time researching to minimize the risk of failure. Compound that with the proliferation of technology choices in the marketplace for almost any category and more time is required to narrow down the field.

In fact, according to recent research, 45% of buyers are spending more time researching purchases, and 45% of buyers are using more sources to research and evaluate purchases. John Dering, senior director of ABM technology and strategy for Demandbase, writes, "People can't just quickly go out and say 'Hey, here's a contract; I want to spend this money; it's in my budget. I want to do it.' They need to understand the return they're going to get on it, as well as the impact it has on the rest of the organization. Those types of things can start to slow down and create a lot more hoops that buyers need to jump through to get to that goal line of making the purchase."[3]

The impact of this trend is that we all have to assume that if a potential buyer has expressed any interest at all, they have most likely done some research already. How much, we can't be sure. But it has likely involved competitors (unless they contacted us as part of their research cycle). Identify and listen for keywords that indicate where your prospects are getting their information.

Understanding the Pack Mentality

You used to be able to sell directly to the C-suite or upper management, and the buying group was relatively small. Now, even CEOs usually won't make a decision on their own without getting input from key stakeholders.

In B2B sales, buyers are social animals, buying in groups. The more stakeholders there are, the harder it gets to make a decision.

---

3   2018 B2B Buyers Survey Report, DemandBase.

The average number of stakeholders getting involved seems to be steadily increasing, making it more and more difficult for the salesperson and the champion to drive alignment across everyone in the group. Why do buyers form groups to make purchasing decisions? Among others, here are a few reasons:

- Better buy-in and adoption post-purchase
- Solutions often touch multiple departments
- Multiple resources are needed from multiple departments to implement the solution
- Budget for the product or solution may have to be cobbled together from multiple department budgets

However, there are several downsides to group buying. Along with normal group dynamics comes group buying dysfunction, which can cause all sorts of hiccups in the purchasing process.

Buying Takes Longer

When was the last time you were part of a large group and tried to decide where to eat for lunch? It takes a lot longer than you expect, doesn't it? And quite often, the decision is based on making sure you don't go to a restaurant that someone doesn't like. So instead of heading for a great restaurant, you head for a mediocre one that at least "doesn't get anyone upset."[4]

This experience describes the risk-averse nature of buyers and the reason it takes so long to make decisions. The larger the group, the harder it is to decide. So while doing more research adds to the buying cycle length, the difficulty of making group decisions is another major factor. Any of us who have been in B2B sales can recognize this truth:

---

4   Consensus, "How is B2B Sales Like Lunch?" YouTube, August 2, 2016, https://www.youtube.com/watch?v=vw36HGBR064.

The larger the group, the longer the deal takes to get done. Calendars are harder to coordinate. Some stakeholders are busier than others. The larger the group, the more misalignment that group will experience and have to work through.

BUYER ENABLEMENT CAN SHORTEN BUYING GROUP TIMELINE

As you facilitate the buying group, the sales cycle naturally gets shorter. In one case, a midmarket software company saw their sales cycle reduce 62%. (See Chapter 15 for more details.)

Increased Confusion over Roles

How many times have you had a prospect tell you, "I'm the decision maker" (and you swallowed that, hook, line, and sinker) only to hear, the day before they are supposed to sign, "Oh, we're ready to sign all right, just as soon as my boss looks this over"? That's when you gulp and realize you're far from getting the deal done.

Increased Risk Aversion

Psychology Today describes Groupthink as when "a group of well-intentioned people make irrational or non-optimal decisions that are spurred by the urge to conform or the discouragement of dissent."[5]

In popular psychology we like to think of Groupthink as a group of individuals making a *more* risky choice because they are in a group, such as a group of teenagers choosing to drive way too fast because they are all together egging each other on. I know I certainly

---

5   "Groupthink," *Psychology Today*, https://www.psychologytoday.com/us/basics/groupthink.

made plenty of stupid choices because of this phenomenon as a child and teenager. From eating live worms and firing bottle rockets into people's open doors when they answered the doorbell, to playing tag in cars at excessive speeds, my youth was filled with decisions that in hindsight were risky and ultimately worked against me. (I suppose there might have been a few wise choices sprinkled in.) At that age, I was unconscious of how the pressure to conform was working against me and my peers' better judgment.

In B2B group purchasing, the opposite holds true: The more people who are in the group, the more risk averse the group becomes. They are more inclined to make a less risky choice that hurts their own group. The main reason for this is that they are trying to make a decision that everyone in the group benefits from, or at least does not object to. The peer pressure to conform becomes the pressure to not make political waves.

This is another aspect of group buying dysfunction: Quite often, the group can benefit from making a purchase, but because as a group they become so risk averse, they choose not to, even though they probably would make the purchase if they were on their own. If you place your champion in the middle of this risk-averse group, you will realize how hard it will be for them to get the group to take a risk on you and your company's solution.

To counter this risk-averse group mentality, you need to head it off at the pass by first warning your champion that they are going to run into this risk aversion. Then you need to provide them with educational information and social proof that will help them understand that the risks are worth taking and likely to result in positive outcomes.

The Challenges of Large Buying Groups

In an article published in the *Harvard Business Review*, the authors state the growing number of stakeholders come from "a lengthening roster of roles, functions, and geographies. The resulting divergence in personal and organizational priorities makes it difficult for buying groups to agree to anything more than 'move cautiously,' 'avoid risk,' and 'save money.' One CMO has memorably referred to this as 'lowest common denominator purchasing.'"[6] In short, for a multitude of reasons, groups tend to be more likely to make poor decisions. Group buying dysfunction is your enemy.

Steal Time from Your Enemy

Have you ever studied timing in sports? I'm a big tennis fan and also play frequently. Roger Federer, arguably the best tennis player who has ever lived, has become a master of stealing time from his opponents. He does it in dozens of ways, but one simple example is by taking the ball on the rise. Most of us wait for the ball to bounce, arc up, then start down before hitting the ball. Instead of waiting, Federer moves into position faster and cranks his forehand while the ball is still on its upward arc, effectively stealing time from his opponents.

Your buyers aren't your opponents, but group buying dysfunction is your enemy. The better you understand your customer and their buying process, the better position you'll be in to steal time from that enemy.

What does that mean? As we discussed earlier, who knows more about how to purchase your product or solution—you or the buyer? You, of course. You have worked through purchases hundreds of times and are familiar with the process. The buyer is only doing this once. Why, then, do you rely on the buyer to tell you what to do next? Shouldn't it be the other way around?

I'm not suggesting you ignore the buyer and discount their input, but you're the expert. You know what typically goes into closing a deal. You know what they need to do to make an effective decision. You know what objections they'll face once they start promoting inside

---

6   Nicholas Toman, Brent Adamson, and Christina Gomez, "The New Sales Imperative," *Harvard Business Review*, March-April, 2017, https://hbr.org/2017/03/the-new-sales-imperative.

their organization. On the other hand, your buyer is blind. And if you let them lead the process without equipping them with the right tools, you'll both get destroyed.

You have to exert buying leadership. You're the experienced combatant. You need to arm your champion for battle. You need to let them know what obstacles they are going to face and give them the tools they need to overcome them.

See the World Through Your Buyer's Eyes

At the core of every buyer is an emotional being who won't decide to make the purchase that you want unless the emotions they care about are satisfied. By either management dictate or by preference, they are going to try to involve others in the decision, leading to larger groups and longer buying cycles.

As a salesperson, it is your responsibility to see the world through your buyers' eyes and understand the dynamics that are influencing their actions and decisions.

CHAPTER 3

WHAT BUYERS WANT

"The only way I can get you to do anything is by giving you what you want."

—DALE CARNEGIE[1]

Sam Levenson said, "Happiness is a by-product. You cannot pursue it by itself." I find that to be true. When I *try* to be happy, I'm not. But when I focus on the things that make me happy and don't think about whether I'm happy, it turns out I am happy. I have never been able to force myself to feel happy. I have to actually do the things that make me happy: Getting wholly engaged in my work. Helping someone in need. Giving someone a sincere compliment. Losing myself playing a competitive game of tennis. Writing. Spending unhurried time with my spouse and children. Creating. Truly listening. Exploring nature, other cultures, or history. Getting lost reading a novel. Praying. And the list goes on.

There is a parallel phenomenon at the root of buyer enablement. I would modify Levenson's quote to "Getting a deal done is a by-product. You cannot pursue it by itself." In other words, the more you focus on

1   Dale Carnegie, *How to Win Friends and Influence People* (New York City: Simon and Schuster, Reissue edition, 2009): 249.

getting the deal done, the harder it becomes. However, the more you focus on meeting the needs of the buyer, the easier it gets.

To meet the needs of the buyer, you have to know what they want. There are seven "buyer wants" that I think are particularly critical for salespeople to understand:

1. To feel heard

2. Authenticity

3. To learn rather than be sold to

4. Self-directed digital access

5. A personalized experience

6. Proof

7. A deal

Buyers Want to Feel Heard

Have you ever been in a purchasing role yourself, whether it was in business or as a consumer, and the salesperson didn't listen to you? How did it affect your desire to do business with that salesperson?

"Seek first to understand, then to be understood."[2] Stephen Covey's ubiquitous business advice from *The 7 Habits of Highly Successful People* is as meaningful today as it has ever been. And it especially applies in sales. Buyers come with needs, pressing needs. Otherwise they would not be talking to you. They want you to become a trusted partner in their journey to achieve their goals or solve their problems. To begin to have an influence on them, your first job is to listen. And this means you have to keep your own statements brief and to the point and then ask key questions. The next time you feel anxious to get a deal done, move your own needs aside and listen.

---

2   Stephen Covey, *The 7 Habits of Highly Successful People* (New York City: Simon and Schuster, 2013): 247.

ACTION TIP

Gartner analyst Michele Buckley states, "Buyers value brevity. At first glance, you may be surprised there are only six sections in the agenda. This is by design, as half of the meeting should be lively discussion, not presentation. It is absolutely essential that you focus on discussion and dialogue to create a compelling value proposition for the individuals in the meeting."[3]

Buyers Want Authenticity

What is it about the traditional stereotype of the used-car salesperson that universally turns people off? It's the lack of authenticity. They don't see the buyer as a person but as a means to hit their number. They don't listen to the buyer; they pressure them. They make buyers feel sold to rather than listened to.

What buyers want is the genuine you. They know you will put your best foot forward and are fine with that. But they want to know you and the company and solution that you represent.

One simple way to show authenticity is to show vulnerability. One of the best ways to do that is to say, "I don't know," when they ask you something you don't know the answer to. Buyers don't expect their sales reps or their solutions to be perfect. What they do want and expect are truly helpful partners who will have their best interests in mind.

When I was a young professional in my early twenties, I had a customer ask if our software did a specific task. I said, "Yes, I think it does." In my mind it seemed obvious that it should do what they were

---

3   Gartner, "Tech Go-to-Market: The Ideal First Sales Meeting Agenda and Presentation," Michele Buckley, January 30, 2018.

asking for, so I assumed it did. When we implemented the product for the customer and they discovered that it did *not* do what I had said it did, they were understandably upset. I told my boss about it, and he helped me set things right with them. Then he said something that helped me for the rest of my days: "Never guess." It's okay to say you don't know and then go find the answer. You don't need to be the expert; you just need to connect them to the expert information that has the answers they are looking for.

Think about your content. Is it authentic and credible? Are you authentic and credible? Part of being authentic is to educate rather than sell.

Buyers Want to Learn Rather than Be Sold To

What is the difference between feeling you are being sold to and feeling you are making an educated purchase decision? There are both stance and process differences.

Buyers almost always engage because they have a problem they want to solve. They need to learn how to solve it. Theoretically you have not only the solutions but also the knowledge of how to solve their problem. The buyer can often tell within minutes of the first engagement what type of salesperson they have on the other line: Is it someone who is trying to sell to them or someone who is trying to educate them?

Sometimes we think our job is to persuade the customer. Instead, focus on educating the customer, and you'll have greater success. As buyers learn, they will feel motivated to take action.

TABLE A: BEING SOLD TO VS. BEING EDUCATED

Being "Sold To"	Being Educated
MINDSET	
My job as a salesperson is to get this deal done. If I don't get this deal done, I won't hit quota. If I don't hit quota, my job might be in jeopardy.	My job as a salesperson is to help the customer solve their problem. If I can gain their trust and solve their problem, they are more likely to buy from me and to refer me to their colleagues and friends.
I need to convince and persuade the prospect this is the best option.	I need to educate the customer so that they choose the option that is best suited for their needs.
I need this deal regardless of whether it's the best fit for the client.	If I find out that this customer isn't suited for our solution, I need to recommend some other places for them to go and move on. There are unlimited opportunities for me to get the deals I need with customers who actually need my solution. The sooner I educate and disqualify the ones who don't need my solution, the sooner I can spend more of my time with those who do need it.
PROCESS	
Ask some questions because I know it's a good sales practice that they taught me and makes the customer feel like I care.	Ask questions because I really do care about the prospect's problems and want to help them solve them.
Present the same thing over and over with a few tweaks.	I listen carefully to what the prospect has to say so that I can make thoughtful recommendations about what to teach them.
Ask the buyer what they think the next steps are because the sooner I follow the steps that the prospect thinks we should follow, the sooner I can get this deal closed.	Having been through the buying process before with many prospects, I know how difficult it can be for the buyer. I make strong recommendations and educate the buyer on why it is important to take them.
I don't ask for commitments because that might make the customer think I'm putting too much burden on them.	I educate the prospect on what needs to happen before we can get the deal done, including pitfalls they are likely to run into, then make recommendations about courses of action, asking for strong commitments from both them and us.

Buyers want to learn how to solve their problems. This involves asking questions to understand what they know and what they don't and then teaching them about how to solve the problem in general and how your product can potentially help. Sell less, educate more, and you'll close more deals.

Buyers Want Self-Directed Digital Access

Ask yourself, "When you go to make a purchase, do you want to engage a salesperson?" If you're responding with "Yes," then ask yourself why. Usually it's something like this: "I want someone who knows how to help me find what I need or choose from a variety of options that all seem similar."

But if you could find that information quickly without having to engage with a salesperson, which would you rather choose?

Most of us would rather choose to find the information on our own, but we engage with salespeople because we think they can more easily find us the information we need.

Is your sales team providing the right kinds of information digitally that your buyers need, and do they know where and how to get it at the time in the buying journey that they need it?

Can your buyers get this information with or without the sales rep?

Some say, "But my prospects want to engage with a live rep, not a digital replacement!" First of all, I'm not advocating that you remove live interaction from the buying process, but I am advocating leveraging digital content in a way that makes it easier for the buyer to get the information they want, then engage with the sales rep when needed. Customers don't have a preference about the channel through which they get the information. What they really want is to get the information that they need when they need it.

Digital Doesn't Mean Helpful

Providing digital information is nothing new. Every company tries to put together relevant information for buyers on their website or through other channels and has been for years now, even decades. So as a whole we ought to be helping buyers pretty effectively today, right? Unfortunately, no!

The first problem is that we produce so much digital information that the prospect doesn't know when or where to access it effectively. To be truly helpful, the "digital sales rep" needs to effectively map the content to the right stage of the buying process and to the right stakeholder and then offer that content at just the right time. Alternatively, technology could use artificial intelligence to determine what stage the buyer is at and do it for you.

Don't Overwhelm

Keep in mind that it's important not to overwhelm the buyer with information. This is why personalization is so important. As you make information accessible online, make sure that there are mechanisms in place for them to get at only the information they need for that stage in the buyer journey.

It's not about the quantity of the information but rather the right amount of information at the right time for the right stakeholder.

Buyers Want a Personalized Experience

I'm sure you've heard the phrase "Show up and throw up." My friend Peter Cohan, author of *Great Demo! How to Create and Execute Stunning Software Demonstrations,* used it as a description of what some sales reps and sales engineers do when meeting with prospects. The salesperson appears and begins telling the prospect all of the reasons why that prospect needs their solution. When they demonstrate the solution, they go through a preplanned demonstration that looks pretty much like the demonstration they just gave to the other prospect the hour before.

Have you ever found yourself sitting through such a demonstration of a product or solution and thinking, *They're not even talking about anything relevant to my needs. What I really want to know is* _____, and just wishing the rep would stop talking so that you can tell them what you really want? I've been in this situation many times myself, and I no longer tolerate it. Instead I interrupt and say, "I'm sorry to interrupt, but I don't really care about this. Here's what I want to know: _____. Can you teach me about that?" If you've ever had a client interrupt you like that, you can bet there are another ten who don't interrupt out of politeness. It's a clear signal that you aren't personalizing the experience for them.

In recent research, 62% of buyers noted a desire for sales to demonstrate experience with or knowledge of their industry.[4] This is one of the reasons many sales teams organize by vertical. One survey respondent put it this way: "[Vendors] could have done a stronger demo that included examples of how we could use the product to meet our unique needs instead of generic examples."

The need to personalize raises some challenges, among them:

- Personalizing at scale: Software as a Service (SaaS) firms who normally sell large deals but are attempting to go down-market, for example, quickly find that the same sales processes that served them up-market don't scale well at the higher volumes necessary.

- Varying levels of skill by reps: This creates very uneven experiences for your prospects and leads to unpredictable sales funnel outcomes.

---

4   "2018 B2B Buyers Survey Report: Sales Representatives Play Greater Role Within Critical 1–3 Month Active Buyer Timeframe," Demand Gen Report, https://www.demandgenreport.com/resources/reports/2018-b2b-buyers-survey-report.

These challenges are another reason for using technology that supports buyer enablement, such as using intelligent demo automation software as a way to automatically personalize some of the education experience to each stakeholder. This moves some of the burden from the individual reps to the technology, making the experience more consistent from rep to rep.

Provide a Special Experience Even During the Buying Process

The buyer's experience during the sales process has at least as much of an impact on getting the deal done as the actual solution itself. In my opinion, this ultimately goes back to trust. If buyers have a great experience during the sales process, you've built trust with them, and they believe that great experience will continue after the deal is signed.

What makes it a great buying experience? Responsiveness, expertise, personalization to their industry and company's unique needs, assertive but tactful leadership, and having their needs anticipated before they state them. Think about the best restaurants and the best hotels or Airbnb locations you've been to. They anticipate what you'll need before you even realize it.

This is why it's so important to immerse yourself in what buyers think, what they want, and how they behave. This is why it is so important to thoughtfully map out the journey you've taken buyers on over and over. Only then will you be able to anticipate the buyers' needs before they realize they have them—which is key to establishing trust and getting to a successful close sooner.

Buyers Want Proof

Most buyers, unless they are very early adopters, want some kind of backup reassuring them that placing their confidence in your product or solution is going to most likely have a happy ending. There are two types of proof that are especially valuable to sellers of technology: social proof and experiential proof.

Social proof comes in the form of online reviews, customer testimonials, case studies, thought leader recommendations, and references. The need for social proof is an effort to reduce risk. Remember from our section on Emotional ROI that the risks are high for buyers, especially the champion(s) leading the purchasing conversation forward.

TECHNOLOGY TIP

When looking for technology that organizes references, testimonials, case studies, and other forms of social proof, look for solutions that can be tagged by industry, company size, and role or title.

Social proof comes in many categories, including:

- White papers
- Case studies
- Quotes
- Video testimonials
- References
- Online review sites

When providing social proof, personalize this as much as possible. If your stakeholder is a C-level executive at a Fortune 1000 company in the manufacturing industry, don't give them a customer testimonial of an end user at a small business in the financial services industry. What a C-level executive wants is a testimonial and case study by other

C-level customers at a similarly large company in the same industry. Where possible, provide five different examples of social proof that are relevant to them over the course of the buying process.

> 42% of buyers listed peers and colleagues as their top source of information, and 67% agreed that they relied more on peer recommendations when making final purchasing decisions.[5]

By experiential proof, I mean that today's B2B buyers want to try before they buy.

At Consensus, we often encourage the buying group to go through what we call a Proof of Value (POV). This takes the traditional Proof of Concept (POC) to the next level.

A POC typically is part of a demonstration where the sales engineering team loads customer data into their platform and customizes the look and feel so that the buying group can get a better idea of how the product applies to them.

In a POV, by contrast, we guide our customers through a mini implementation, essentially a pilot project, to prove value before a larger purchase is made. Obviously this is only useful if you are confident your solution will provide value during a short time period with a few users. If not, the POV may need to include many users and go as long as a year.

At ADP, a company well known for its payroll software, one presales team that was evaluating our interactive video demo software to help them scale their presales function initially purchased licenses for a group of only 50 presales reps. Part of their objective was to scale

---

5   "2017 B2B Buyers Survey Report," Demand Gen,
     https://www.demandgenreport.com/resources/research/2017-b2b-buyers-survey-report.

down-market, where volume is higher and deal sizes are smaller. This had put increasing demand for demos on the presales team.

After using interactive video demos for a few months and seeing how deals began to close with fewer requests for demos from the presales team, including one deal closing with no requests for live demos at all, ADP requested quotes for more licenses.

Find a way to help your buyers try before they buy, and they'll buy more and more often.

Give Them a Demo

Think about the last time you bought a car. Would you have purchased it without a demonstration first? In the car buying process, the test drive is the demo. Often a salesperson accompanies you to point out specific features and benefits.

SaaS buyers are the same. Not only do they *want* to see how your solution works; they also *need* to see how it works if they are to be effective ambassadors for your solution. Think of your own software-purchasing behavior—going back to buyer empathy again. Surely you wanted a demo the last time you purchased a software product. So if we want a demo when we buy software, we shouldn't be surprised that B2B buyers want demos of our products.

Value assessment tools, such as ROI and total cost of ownership (TCO) calculators, can help buying teams better articulate the benefits of investing in a type of solution. A great demo, while often conducted in a controlled environment, still offers a good "window" into the real capabilities and values that a TSP (Technology and Service Provider) can offer. And a customer telling the story is almost always more credible than the TSP telling the same story. This dynamic is also driving the increasing buyers' expectation to be able to use a free trial version of the product.[6]

I have found that vendors are reluctant to provide a demo too early in the purchase process, often for good reason. When vendors provide a feature-rich demo early in the purchasing process, it often backfires with buyers getting bogged down in details that aren't relevant early in the purchasing process before a clear picture of value creation is established.

The key is to have different types of demos prepared to meet customer needs at different stages of their buying process. There are really four different types of demos—vision, qualifying, solution, and closing—that I'll discuss in depth later. For now, just remember that having your prospects fully learn about and *experience* your solution's benefits will be a powerful tool for swaying their choice in your direction.

Technology can help both automate each of these demo types so prospects can get access to the demo when they are ready and make the experience customizable to the specific individual watching them.

Buyers Want a Deal

A friend of mine, who is a Global SVP of Inside Sales for a large IT security software firm, told me excitedly one day, "I just got $2 million worth of software for $1 million!"

What struck me was how much the "bargain" meant to him. He felt like he had just won a coup for his company and his team. Getting such a good deal from the vendor also stroked his ego. He could continue to think of himself as a good negotiator.

Also not lost on me was the fact that the software company on the

6   Gartner, *Trust Drives the B2B Technology Customer Life Cycle*, Carrie Cowan, Hank Barnes, Maria Marino, December 5, 2019.

other side had just inked a $1 million deal, which I knew for that company was a big opportunity.

Even though price is not the factor that matters most to buyers, everyone loves a deal. While it's important to protect your price point and deal size, start at a place where you can offer the buyer something special. Many buyers hold out until they think they are getting a deal, so if you want to speed up the buying process, offer them something that can help them feel like they are getting a bargain.

The key is to always get something else in return. It could be more licenses if they close by a certain time, or a discount on price if they sign a multiyear contract. Sometimes the "deal" doesn't have to be in the form of discounts but rather in the pricing model. Try offering different pricing models instead of discounting.

At one of my previous companies, we began offering two pricing models: a typical user-based model and an alternative "number of active projects" model with unlimited users. Getting unlimited users felt like a deal to certain customers. The active projects model encouraged usage and adoption. In either model, we had really good margins, so we didn't care which they chose.

Again, this goes to personalizing the experience. Offering different pricing models to choose from will help them feel catered to, and they'll be less likely to require as much discounting because you're meeting other needs.

There is a lot written about how to protect price. My focus here is on what the buyer wants: some kind of deal that they can feel good about. Getting a deal is part of the Emotional ROI.

Fulfill Customer Wants

If you look carefully at the list of wants in this chapter, you may notice a common thread: All of them relate to the Emotional ROI that I discussed in Chapter 2. If you work on filling these wants, your buyers will have an easier time overcoming their emotional reluctance to making a decision, so the logic of why your solution is the best choice for them can win the day.

When logic and emotion come together, prospects will almost always agree to a deal with you (assuming you have a viable solution). However, that doesn't mean rolling over or giving discounts. It simply means that you need to anticipate what they want and plan it into your sales processes ahead of time so that you can anticipate their needs and give it to them before they're even asking. By giving them what they want, you'll get what you want: a profitable deal done quickly.

CHAPTER 4

WHAT BUYERS *NEED* FROM *YOU*

"Whoever is careless with the truth in small matters cannot be
trusted with important matters."

—ALBERT EINSTEIN

We know that buyers want proof, but are we aware that the kind of proof they're looking for is evidence that you really are customer focused, that you really are trying to look at issues through their eyes, that you really are concerned about meeting their needs, that you really are trying to help them move through the buying process? They are looking for reasons to trust you.

There are many items that could fit into this category, but let's focus on the following six that I think are the most effective in providing the proof of your commitment. Buyers need:

1. Your responsiveness

2. Reasons to trust you

3. Coaches, not sellers

4. Their concerns resolved and questions answered

5. ROI at every touch point

6. To know you're with them *after* the purchase

Buyers Need Responsiveness

Last summer, I needed my sprinklers repaired. I called four different sprinkler repair shops and left messages. Not one got back to me. I called again. Still no response. Finally, weeks later, I received a phone call from one of the vendors: "Hi, we saw that you left a message. We're really booked up, but how can we help you?" Do you think I gave them my business? Not a chance. I eventually asked for referrals and found a sprinkler vendor that responded within minutes every time I reached out for help or questions.

As much as buyers want you and your solution to be competent and able to help them, they want to know that you are sincerely interested in helping them. The first indication is your responsiveness.

In Demand Gen's "Buyer Report 2017," 97% of buyers cited "timeliness of a vendor's response to inquiries" as an important aspect of the purchasing process.[1] That is virtually every buyer.

Responsiveness comes in many forms, but here are a few actions you can take:

- Quickly return calls and emails
- Promptly deliver what you have committed to deliver
- Provide them access to helpful information for their stage in the journey, including a product demo when they want it rather than waiting to deliver it when you think they are ready
- Have an answer for pricing when they ask for it rather than putting it off
- Quickly track down answers to questions or concerns
- Send calendar invites quickly
- Arrive at meetings early so you're never in a rush or late

---

1 "2017 B2B Buyers Survey Report," Demand Gen,
   https://www.demandgenreport.com/resources/research/2017-b2b-buyers-survey-report.

TIP

Where possible, engage your prospects with technology that makes responsiveness easier. If they'll let you text them directly, choose that over email where it makes sense. Or invite them and other key stakeholders to an instant chat channel, such as Slack or Zoom, where you and the buying group can all turn things around quickly without having to schedule a call.

Buyers Need Reasons to Trust You

Buyers want to trust you, but they've been through so many purchasing situations where their trust was either never won or was eroded that they usually start from a position of mistrust.

Imagine that you tell a prospect, "Sure, I'll get that white paper out to you today." Then your biggest client calls. After that, your spouse asks you to be home early so they can make an appointment they had forgotten about. Then your boss texts you asking for a report to be delivered earlier than you expected. Suddenly you have forgotten about your prospect, and when you remember them, you tell yourself, "I'll just have to get it to them tomorrow."

Here's the same scene from the buyer's perspective: You said you would get the white paper out to them today, and you didn't.

But it doesn't stop there. If that pattern continues, the buyer begins to think, sometimes subconsciously, *If the salesperson can't deliver what they commit to when promised, I'm beginning to doubt the company can deliver on its promises.*

I was talking to Jed Morley, an expert at brand strategy and messaging and a friend of mine, and he summed up branding as "Promises made. Promises kept." It may seem like a small thing, but those small things add up to either building trust or eroding trust in not only you but also your company and brand.

In my experience, customers often want and even expect more functionality than currently exists after the purchase. In other words, there is a gap in expectation fulfillment.

Why does this happen? As salespeople, we sometimes have a tendency to overpromise on features to help get the deal done. This leads to dissatisfaction and regret on the part of the buyer. Instead of letting this happen, ask yourself, "Do I keep my word 100% of the time to my buyers?" If not, make some adjustments.

If you're a sales leader, ask yourself, "What can I do to inculcate a culture of honesty, dependability, and trust on my team?" It starts with you and how you follow through with your team members. Do you keep your word to them? By extension, they will begin to do this more and more with the prospects they work with.

Trust is developed not only by keeping your word and staying true to what your product can actually do (and not do) but also by the quality and usefulness of the interactions and information that you provide.

According to Gartner, "As buyers get deeper into their buying journey, the TSPs (Technology and Service Providers) that they continue to evaluate have more opportunities to interact directly with the buying team. These interactions—whether they are meetings, demonstrations, or project discussions—carry a bigger trust impact as the decision-making effort progresses. The more these interactions demonstrate contextual understanding of the buying team's situation, the more trust grows."[2]

---

2   Gartner, *Trust Drives the B2B Technology Customer Life Cycle*, Carrie Cowan, Hank Barnes, Maria Marino, December 5, 2019.

BUILDING TRUST

To enable the buyer, we first need to win their trust. To win their trust, we must:

- Listen and inquire sincerely
- Actually care and not think of them as numbers or objects
- Follow through on our commitments (i.e., keep our word)
- Demonstrate that we know how to speak to them and potentially solve their problems
- Respond quickly to their needs
- Point them to a different solution if they aren't the right fit for ours
- Never overstate the capabilities of our product or solution
- Provide quality helpful content at the right times
- Never disparage the competition even while we put our best foot forward

For more tips on how to win buyer trust, see Chapter 5.

Buyers Need Coaches, Not Sellers

Considering the complexity of making B2B purchases, buyers need coaches, or guides, through the journey rather than someone trying to convince them their solution is the best solution for them. We need to change our mentality as salespeople and consider ourselves as service-oriented participants in a complex problem-solving process. The more we take this approach, the more likely we will be to secure the trust of the buyers and help them solve their problems, which means a deal for us.

This also means that we do need to have, or have at our disposal, an array of tools and information to help the buyer. If you aren't experienced enough, you'll need to bring others in to help you coach the buyer.

So who are you coaching and on what topics? The main person or people you'll coach are your champions. They are your internal team working to get your deal done inside their target organization. What to coach on varies over time. Here are some of the key issues that you'll need to coach your champions on:

- The competitive landscape and where your solution fits in, what kinds of situations your competition's solutions are useful for, and the unique situations and problems that your solution solves
- Things to consider as they try to solve the problem with the solution that you're offering
- Steps in the purchasing process
- Commitments you and they will need to make to have a successful completion
- What roles usually need to get involved and why
- What stage in the buying process each role gets involved
- What questions or concerns are usually raised by what roles
- What materials and informational resources you have to help address those concerns or questions and when to use them
- How successful customers implement your solution and what other stakeholders need to get involved after the purchase

Buyers Need Their Concerns Resolved

At some point in the buyer journey, they are going to have questions and concerns. They won't move forward without having them resolved. Using the buyer enablement approach, we don't wait for these concerns to come up; instead we move proactively to resolve them ahead of time.

In war, a preemptive strike is a surprise attack used to counter an anticipated enemy offensive. If you know your enemy is going to strike, it might be wise to take out their ability to do so before that happens.

In my opinion, late-stage objections are the enemy. "Resolving 'all concerns and objections' to move forward with a solution (or abandon the process entirely) is likely to take buyers 2.6 months. Technology buyers spend on average 16.3 months to complete a new IT purchase."[3]

The key is to anticipate what your buyers' concerns will be and take action *before* they surface. The beautiful thing is that you, or your sales team collectively, already know almost all of the concerns that will likely come up. Why? Because you've all been through enough buying engagements that you know what questions come up and where the obstacles are.

Buyers Need ROI at Every Touch Point, Not Just at the End

Sometimes we think of return on investment (ROI) in terms of the endgame: What will the buyer get in the final analysis? Andy Paul, founder of The Sales House and author of several business books on sales, including *Amp Up Your Sales*, suggests that we need to think of ROI every time we engage with a customer.

To do this, think of the final ROI as the accumulation of small ROIs over time. Andy calls these "moments that make a difference." He encourages salespeople to ask the following question: "What is the ROI for the buyer from this sales touch?" In other words, if a buyer is going to invest their time with you, even for a few minutes, what do they get out of it? Andy's recommendation is that we "define and deliver a value plan for every call."

---

3   Gartner, *Tech Go-to-Market: Why Tech Sales Cycles Are Taking So Long and What Needs to Be Done Now*, Michelle Buckley, June 4, 2018.

"Define and deliver a value plan for every call." —ANDY PAUL, THESALESHOUSE.COM

The ability to deliver small pieces of ROI as moments that make a difference goes back to buyer empathy. You need to focus on where each buyer is in the process and what they need to know or decide in order to move on to the next step. The buyer must come away with value from every interaction with you, or they won't see any point in continuing the process.

Peter Cohan, author of *Great Demo!*, specifically encourages this kind of thinking for those customer calls and roles where the value to the buyer is often overlooked, such as with business development representatives (BDRs). Sometimes called sales development representatives (SDRs), these early stage sales roles who set appointments for more experienced account executives are often filled with young, inexperienced talent.

"Most BDR conversations have practically no value to me as a customer and even border on coming across as rude," Peter told me. I think most of us can relate. Contrary to popular approaches, Peter recommends putting your highest level, most knowledgeable (rather than your lowest level, least knowledgeable) reps on qualification calls.

At the core of the problem in this situation is the BDR's focus. They don't exhibit "buyer empathy." They are thinking about trying to get the buyer to do or say what the BDR wants them to say. Instead they need to think about the call as an investment in time and attention and ask, "What can I provide of value?"

In short, you're never going to get to an endgame ROI if you don't deliver value throughout the process. The buyer will dump you, often after the first call or outreach. On the other hand, if you deliver value every time they engage with you, they'll keep coming back, clear through the close and then through the renewal subscription.

Buyers Need to Know You're with Them *After* the Purchase

Imagine that you have taken a journey deep into the rain forest. Your guide has navigated you through the toughest situations, and through it all you have arrived at your destination: a tribe that has largely been untouched by civilization. You're shown to your hut. You go in, organize your gear, and then go out to see what is next. All of a sudden, your guide disappears into the thicket, and you're left there in the middle of a tribe you're completely unfamiliar with and wondering how you'll ever get out of this alive.

Does this sound familiar? To many buyers, it is all too familiar. Too often in sales, we get the deal done and move on without making an effective handoff. This reveals the sales mindset rather than the buyer mindset. If you have a buyer mindset, you intuitively recognize that they need help.

Not only do we need to make sure we are there for them during the transition to the customer success team, but we also need to forecast that up front. Buyers want to know before the deal is done how implementation, training, and customer support works. They want to know who will be taking care of them.

I love this stage of the buying process because in the process of discussing and educating the buyer on what will happen after the deal gets done and planning with them how they'll arrive at the value they are making the purchase for in the first place, you are in effect getting a presumptive close. They would not be discussing implementation details with you if they weren't planning on getting a deal done.

My recommendation is to introduce the prospect to the client-success manager, who will work with them long before the deal gets done. It helps the client recognize that you are trying to educate rather than sell while at the same time building trust in the organization's competence.

Your Actions Build Trust

All of the "need from you" tips in this chapter link back to the idea that your mindset needs to switch from "making a sale" to "helping a customer buy." If you are responsive to your customers, if you give them reasons to trust you by virtue of what you say and do, if you act in the role of a coach, if you make sure their concerns are resolved and make sure they continually gain value in working with you (during and after the sale), then you will create a path for buying groups that makes it easier for them to move more quickly through their buying steps. And because they trust your authentic commitment to them, they are more likely to stay loyal to you and your company.

CHAPTER 5

SALES SKILLS KEY TO BUYER ENABLEMENT

"Human behavior flows from three main sources:
desire, emotion, and knowledge."

—PLATO

In Ben Horowitz's landmark book for entrepreneurs, *The Hard Thing About Hard Things,* he shares a story about his VP of sales doing a deal review with his team:

> We held a weekly forecast call where Mark reviewed every deal in front of the entire 150 person sales force. On one such call, a salesperson described an account that he'd forecast in detail: "I have buy-in from my champion, the vice president that he reports to, and the head of purchasing. My champion assures me that they'll be able to complete the deal by the end of the fiscal quarter.
>
> Mark quickly replied, "Have you spoken to the vice president's peer in the networking group?"
>
> Sales rep: "Um, no I haven't."

Mark: "Have you spoken to the vice president yourself?"

Sales rep: "No."

Mark: "Okay, listen carefully. Here's what I'd like you to do. First, reach up to your face and take off your rose-colored glasses. Then get a Q-tip and clean the wax out of your ears. Finally, . . . call the [expletive] vice president right now, because you do not have a deal."

Mark was right. It turned out that we did not have a deal, as the vice president's peer in networking was blocking it. We eventually got a meeting with him and won the deal.[1]

That VP had guided enough buyer groups through the buying journey to know whether the deal was on track or not. He knew which stakeholders needed to get involved, what pitfalls were likely to happen, and what had to be done to help the buyers overcome their own dysfunction. (Also interesting to note is that the champion did not know the deal was at risk. Remember, like Mark, you really should know more about how the buying process works than your prospect!)

There are certain selling skills that are critical for successful buyer enablement. Mastering these skills will help make sure you don't get caught flat-footed like the salesperson in Horowitz's story.

Lead with Strength and Conviction

Blogger Jonathan Sandling writes that as humans we thrive under real leadership for three reasons:

- Survival: avoiding threats
- Purpose: Why am I here?

---

1 Ben Horowitz, *The Hard Thing About Hard Things: Building a Business When There Are No Easy Answers* (New York City: HarperBusiness, 2014): 50.

- Achievement: success and rewards[2]

Our buyers want to be led in these three areas as they explore our solution.

Remember, we're no longer sellers first. We're aware of the emotional risks our champion is taking to reap the rewards of implementing our solution. We want them to go through this journey successfully. So we're guides, coaches, and trusted mentors. These are all titles worthy of our experience and knowledge, as we've already taken dozens, maybe hundreds, of buyers through the journey.

Salespeople know more about buying processes than their customers do because they go through the buying process over and over again with each new sale. Prospects and buyers may experience the process only once or twice. That's why a key skill for salespeople is learning how to be a leader of buying who can guide their prospects through the process without seeming to take over.

To clarify, exerting leadership doesn't mean we should stop asking questions. In the Amazon jungle expedition analogy, you might ask questions like, "What is most important to you on this expedition: safety or excitement?" Or "Are you most interested in learning about the jungle, its peoples, or the geography?" Or "If you could have one story to tell when you're done with this expedition, what would it be?" Getting the answers to these questions would help you know what choices you should make at key points in the journey.

Similarly, asking probing questions to deeply understand your prospect's needs up front is critical to knowing what to recommend on the buying journey as you move forward. But my point is for you to exert that leadership: Recommend. Strongly recommend. Explain why. Then ask them for commitments and expect them to follow through. That is leadership, and buyers not only want it but also need it.

Some salespeople assume that if they try to exert strong leadership, they'll come across as too pushy, which results in salespeople waiting for the prospect to guide the journey, almost always resulting in disaster.

2   Jonathan Sandling, "3 Reasons Why We Need Leaders" (blog), August 21, 2014, https://jonathansandling.com/3-reasons-why-we-need-leaders.

In fact, the opposite is true. Salespeople who tactfully exert strong leadership in the sales process come across as helpful. Exerting strong leadership helps build trust. Buyers want to know that you know how to help them achieve their objectives.

Identify and Connect with Key Decision Makers

What is one of the key differentiators between world-class sales performers and the rest of the field? World-class performers get access to key decision makers. How often? In one report, almost always. In other surveys from 2015 and 2016, the top performers gained access to the needed decision makers 85%–90% of the time.[3]

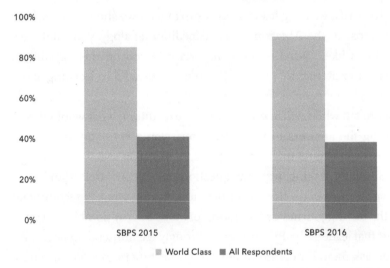

IN A LARGE DEAL, WE ALWAYS
GAIN ACCESS TO KEY DECISION MAKERS

■ World Class ■ All Respondents

Figure 9: Access to Key Decision Makers: This chart shows the difference between what the best sales people do compared to average sales reps: reach more key decision makers.

---

3   Tamara Schenk, "How to Gain Access to Key Decision Makers: What World-Class Performers Do Differently" CSO Insights, blog, July 14, 2016, https://www.csoinsights.com /blog/how-to-gain-access-to-key-decision-makers-what-world-class-performers-do-differently/.

As Tamara Schenk of CSO Insights puts so clearly, "Imagine you are traveling with your laptop and your smartphone. For some reason, you are stuck in the desert, and you have no Wi-Fi connection whatsoever. It means you have no access. No access to emails; no access to information you are used to gathering from various websites, no access to your network where you could ask for help. Now, imagine you are working on a large deal, and you have no access to the key decision makers. It feels almost like being in the desert with no Wi-Fi."[4]

Tamara goes on to say, "Identifying the key decision makers in a large deal is the first step. Social media can help a lot to speed up this process. Then, this group of decision makers has to be analyzed to figure out what value means for each of them based on their role, position, and specific responsibilities."

DON'T FORGET THE SECONDARY STAKEHOLDERS

Quite often sales teams think they have everyone involved to get a deal done but forget they still need to get through finance, IT, and legal. While these stakeholder roles in the buying group don't necessarily have a big say in whether or not your solution can help their organization achieve their goals, they are there to mitigate risk. They may not be able to get the deal done for you, but they can kill your deal.

Make sure to involve these secondary stakeholders as early as possible. Even before you get a verbal commitment from your champion or the buying group, begin educating your champion on what usually has to happen with these secondary stakeholders to get the deals through in their type of organization. Ask your champion to begin finding out who they will need to engage in these different areas so that when the time comes, you don't spend precious purchasing cycle time rounding up these connections.

---

4   Schenk, "How to Gain Access to Key Decision Makers."

Identify Customers' Readiness to Become Buyers

How often have you encountered a lead in a sales conversation who asked for a demo, and you think that because of this request they are far along in the buying cycle? But then you meet with them only to discover that they wanted the demo just to get educated on "what is out there." In other words, at this point they aren't thinking about you as a vendor or even about solving a problem that your solution addresses.

Another way to put it is that buyers are always thinking but rarely about your domain, you as a vendor, or any of the myriad things that you think about. Most buyers are technically not even buyers yet— they are just people in early stages of learning and becoming aware.

"Gartner has identified that buyers will be in one of four states of readiness at the time of first contact with a TSP—whether it be initiated by the TSP or the buyer:

- Unaware—Triggered by a topic that sounds interesting, this state occurs when buying teams are not yet even thinking about a technology-driven opportunity for improvement.

- Aware—Buying teams are aware of the improvement opportunity but are not at a point where they have prioritized this highly, so they are not ready to buy.

- Shopping—Buying teams are ready to buy but have not decided on the exact provider, or set of providers, to select.

- Buying—Buying teams are ready to buy and know who they prefer to purchase from."[5]

Consider that every stakeholder who joins the buying group in effect has to go through the first three states before they are ready to buy. Also note that for a prospect to become your champion, they need to

---

5   Gartner, "Use Situational Messaging to Improve Customer Engagement," Ray Pun, July 22, 2019.

progress to at least the shopping state and likely the buying state. They will help the rest of the buying group go through these states. Before each conversation, make it a goal to assess your buyer's readiness.

One of the best ways to know a buyer's readiness is to closely observe what your contacts will commit to do and what they actually do. The best indicator of the state of a deal is not the sales actions you've taken or what the buyers tell you; it's the *buyers' actions* that tell you the unvarnished truth about the health and speed of the deal.

As you understand where the prospect is in the buying process, you can tailor your content more specifically. For example, Peter Cohan, author of *Great Demo!*, advises to start all customer conversations with "the last thing first,"[6] meaning talk with the customer about what they want to achieve, about a meaningful outcome, before talking with them about how they can get there. Depending on where the customer is at, the last thing first might be quite different.

- If the buyer's state of readiness is unaware, the last thing first might be the problem the customer in the case study is facing, because that will resonate the most.

- If the buyer's state of readiness is aware, the last thing first is probably the outcome of implementing a solution to the problem.

- If you're using the case study to discover where the buyer is at, pause regularly to find out what, if anything, in the customer story resonates with your prospect.

---

6   Peter Cohan, *Great Demo! How to Create and Execute Stunning Software Demonstrations*, 2nd edition (Bloomington, IN: iUniverse, 2005): 1.

TECHNOLOGY TIP

One of the perks of bringing technology into the selling process is that you do not have to wait until you engage *in person* with the buyer to evaluate where they are in the process. Your digital content and underlying technology should allow you to ask questions and observe how your buyers engage with the content. Having this data before the call is, as one of my company's customers put it, "like having the answers to the test beforehand."

Buyers Are Ready to Make Commitments

Buyers not only want to trust you but also want to have the reputation of being trusted or trustworthy. In sales, this takes the form of following through on commitments they make to you. Too often we think we need to do all of the work in the buying process, but to get a deal done, commitments must be followed through on both sides.

If you find out a prospect isn't ready for commitments, then they aren't really *buyers* yet. By asking for commitments, you'll not only increase their trust in you but also quickly uncover those prospects who are exploring but aren't buying.

So start asking for commitments, especially when *you* are making commitments (and following through). Here are some examples:

- "I'll see if we can get this Proof of Value moving forward. Will you go and see if you can get budget allocated based on the assumption that we can demonstrate value?"

- "I'm excited to work with you as you explore our solution. I commit to helping you quickly with everything you need to make a confident purchasing decision. Will you commit to getting a purchasing decision done by the end of this quarter?"

Asking for commitments from the buyer not only moves the buying process along but also establishes that you are an experienced, confident professional who knows how to move the process forward.

COMMITMENTS ARE THE LITMUS TEST FOR PROGRESS

If a buyer balks at making a commitment, you know they aren't quite ready to move forward in the buying process. What is the best way to find out where a deal is at, whether it is real and progressing or not? Ask for a commitment and see if the buyer accepts it and follows through. If they are hesitant, ask them why.

Sell the Pain of Change

What do you sell? Is it a product? A solution? No matter what you actually sell, I can tell you this: What you really sell is the pain of change. Think about it. If you're selling a new product, you're telling the customer that the process of learning to use and implement your product will eventually (and hopefully sooner rather than later) be less painful than what they are currently doing. If you're selling services, you are asking your buyer to believe that the pain of developing a new relationship with you as a service provider is going to be less than either a previous service provider or their internal process.

Another way to think about this is that selling Emotional ROI needs to be embedded in everything we do as salespeople. As discussed, the first step is to recognize that, just like consumers, B2B buyers make purchases for emotional reasons. Once we know that, every touch point needs to reinforce a buyer's belief that the Emotional ROI will be worth it—and by big margins.

Reinforcing this belief is a balancing act of mitigating emotional risk. Let's start with offering a good product, the first step in effec-tively selling Emotional ROI. Here are four tactics you can use to accomplish this.

Tactic 1: Ask Compelling Questions About Emotional ROI

Asking questions during the sales process that make prospects really think about all the issues involved in the purchase and implementa-tion will help you and the prospect know if your solution is truly going to work for them.

Sometimes, salespeople avoid asking tough questions because we are afraid of the answers we may receive. We don't want to consider, for example, that this may not be the best time for the client to imple-ment. But wouldn't you rather get the deal done and implemented when it makes sense for the client instead of forcing them into an implementation too early and ending up with an unhappy customer that is just going to churn the next year?

Here are some examples of questions you might consider asking to help a customer evaluate their own Emotional ROI:

- Do you have other big projects already underway that could get in the way of implementing this solution?

- Who else needs to get in on this purchase to make sure every-one who needs to have a say has it?

- Based on our experience with other clients, this implementa-tion and adoption is going to take 15 hours of your time over the next two weeks and 90 hours of combined time by all involved in implementation over the next four weeks. Will you and oth-ers be able to devote the time necessary to work with our team to get this going?

- Now that you understand what it will take to get this solution implemented, what seems more challenging: the downsides of your current solution or the effort required to get a solution like this in place?

- What is top of mind for you next month and next quarter? Can you make this a priority? Given the value that we've established, are there other projects you could postpone to make sure we can get this going?

Again, these are tough questions. But it's much better to ask them up front than it is to discover, after a client has already purchased your solution, that they simply don't have the time or resources needed to implement it.

At Consensus, we call this focus on the post-sale deployment during the purchasing process "selling for the renewal."

KICKSTART EMOTIONAL ROI WITH GOOD DESIGN

We live in what I call the Age of Design. You may have heard the mantra "Life is too short for bad software." Poor product design significantly reduces Emotional ROI.

If you're selling software, your clients may be spending several hours per day or week interacting with your software design. They may even spend more time with your software than with their spouse or friends. Knowing this, they must believe that they will enjoy using your solution or product more than their current solution, if they have one.

It's not just about the outcome or about what the services themselves will do. It's about the experience buyers have while they are using your product and while they are engaging with your services. It's not good enough for your client to love everything about your software's output if it looks like it's going to be a pain to use.

That said, what do you do if you have no control over product design? (Most of us don't.) I suggest not complaining about it but

continued

recognizing that this will be a mathematical factor in how they calculate Emotional ROI. You have to become extra skilled at educating prospects on the benefits of your solution.

Salesforce CRM, for almost two decades, had one of the most poorly designed pieces of software ever made, but they still became the largest SaaS company in the world by helping prospects believe in the value that would far outweigh the pain of using their poorly designed UI.

Tactic 2: Double Down on the Pain of the Status Quo

All B2B sales should start with the pain point you're solving, but you need to evaluate whether the prospect sees the pain as a mosquito bite or a shark bite. In a lot of cases, they have lived with the pain of the status quo for so long that they don't recognize how big of a pain point it really is. If it's a shark bite and they think it's a mosquito bite, you need to work to help them recognize that.

For the prospect to purchase, they have to believe that the pain of the status quo is greater than the pain of change. The more you can help them feel the pain of the status quo, the bigger the push for Emotional ROI.

Tactic 3: Minimize Risks to Peer Reputation

A buyer wants to know how what you are selling will increase their reputation with their peers. We don't recommend that you address this concern overtly, at least not in your first conversation. Marketing materials can be useful here because they can make claims that border on outrageous if spoken in person. "Be the hero . . ." or "You'll be a rock star . . ." are messages you'll see from time to time, addressing this particular emotional risk.

One of the best ways to minimize risk to a buyer's peer reputation is to provide social proof by way of peer reviews on sites like G2 Crowd or Capterra, as well as great customer references. And don't just provide general references. Provide peer-driven references that are relevant to each of the roles in the buying group. For example, if you're selling a solution to marketing, but the CTO is concerned about security, give the CTO the names of a few other CTOs at client companies.

Hearing another CTO say that your software passed his company's security review with flying colors will go a long way toward a new buyer believing that they will also have a successful implementation. If a CTO, CMO, and head of sales are in the buying group, provide them with peer references from customers who are in similar roles.

Tactic 4: Enhance Upward Mobility

Understand your prospects' immediate goals. What are they trying to achieve this month? Quarter? Year? If you can demonstrate that your solution gets them to their goals faster or better, they'll believe it will help them be more upwardly mobile in their careers.

This is where the financial or productivity ROI becomes emotional. If prospects believe you can deliver the key business metrics that determine their performance, they will consciously (and subconsciously) associate your solution with upward mobility.

Make sure to get the buyer's manager or boss involved too. They are likely going to get involved behind the scenes either way, so proactively involving them up front increases your chances of helping them commit to the purchasing decision. This ultimately increases the upward mobility opportunity for your prospect.

Map Out the Buying Process (and Educate Your Buyers)

Buyers want to be in control, or at least feel like it. This means that when it comes to the buying process, you need to map out the journey for them. When buyers begin the buyer journey, they don't know what they are getting themselves into. They are most focused on the problem they are trying to solve and quite often are also focused on what solving the problem is going to do for their careers. They are quite oblivious to the complexity they are about to immerse themselves in.

Buyers don't know where to begin, what the pitfalls might be, what paths they should be considering and avoiding, or how to arrive at their destination. But you do. You and your sales team have watched buyers take this journey over and over.

"I think ultimately buyers want a process that makes them feel in control, that is easy to access and continue at their pace," says Greg Holmes, a presales leader at software company Flexera whom I interviewed.

The more we explain and educate around the process they need to go through, the more in control they will feel. Again, we need to stop asking the buyer, "What do you think the next steps are?" Instead, we need to exert leadership and recommend to them what the next steps are based on our experience and then ask for their commitment.

Mapping out what is required for each role helps customers plan appropriately, reducing their emotional risk and increasing their Emotional ROI. Providing data from past client engagements gives new buying groups even more confidence in your projected time investment.

This also helps prospects understand how much time they may have to sacrifice from family, friends, and hobbies to get the benefits they want from your solution.

Deployment time is becoming as equally important to buyers as the price tag. 80% of buyers rank deployment . . . as very important, when compared with 75% who ranked price as very important.[7]

Provoke a Change in the Buyer's Mind

One of your constant battles is persuading your prospect to switch from the status quo to your solution. We all recognize that for a buyer to switch products or solutions, they need to see more value in your solution than in their current one. However, most salespeople simply highlight the discrepancy (or gap) in features, functionality, or benefits for the customer. We think, *It will be obvious we have a better solution, so who would not want to change?*

But research demonstrates that highlighting the gap alone doesn't actually change people's minds—that's impossible. But you can help them change their own minds, and research suggests that using a technique called *upward counterfactual thinking* could have a big impact.

Counterfactual thinking is replaying an alternate reality about the past. Upward counterfactual thinking is imagining what we could have done differently to achieve our desired result.

Counterfactual thinking is simply replaying an alternate reality about the past. "If I had done X, then Y may have resulted." There are two types of counterfactual thinking: downward and upward (also called "additive" in some studies).

A downward counterfactual is looking at alternate realities that

---

7   "2017 B2B Buyers Survey Report," Demand Gen,
     https://www.demandgenreport.com/resources/research/2017-b2b-buyers-survey-report.

might have been worse. For example, suppose we get caught in a traffic jam because of an accident and are five minutes late for a sales visit on-site. Because we're late, the appointment has to be rescheduled. Our first thought might be negative as we experience the disappointment of not getting to meet with the customer. However, if we tell ourselves the following story, we might feel better: "Oh, I'm glad I got here five minutes late. I saw that accident. That might have been me if I had been on time." In other words, we tell ourselves a story about what might have happened to make our lives worse. An article titled "The Benefit of Counterfactual Thinking" in *Psychology Today* suggests that downward counterfactuals help improve our moods but don't improve our future performance.[8] In this scenario we are just as likely to be late for our next sales appointment.

Upward counterfactuals, in contrast, are scenarios we run in our minds that could have changed the current outcome to be more favorable. We might say to ourselves, "You can't ever tell what traffic you're going to encounter. I need to get on the road sooner. If I had just gotten out of bed 20 minutes earlier, I would have been able to meet with the prospect and probably would have closed the deal already."

Research suggests that this kind of upward counterfactual thinking (where we imagine what we could have done differently to achieve our desired result) causes discomfort or tension but actually improves future performance. In other words, if we think of it that way, we are more likely to get out of bed earlier and make it on time to the next appointment.

Applying Upward Counterfactual Thinking

So, let's apply upward counterfactual thinking to influencing our buyers to switch from the current solution to our own solution, if not now, in the future.

---

8   PT Staff, "The Benefit of Counterfactual Thinking," *Psychology Today*, July 1, 1995, https://www.psychologytoday.com/us/articles/199507/the-benefit-counterfactual-thinking.

Citing research, ChangingMinds.org suggests the following coun-terintuitive guidance: "Cause tension . . . then offer a new thought that can replace the uncomfortable thought. Encourage them to accept the new thought 'What if you had . . . ?'"[9]

So how can we apply this in a sales scenario where we encounter an entrenched competitor? First, cause tension, discomfort, or disso-nance. Ask questions about their current efforts that challenge the status quo. Help them focus on the things they don't like about the current solution. For example, "What problems are you experiencing with your current solution?"

Using this first step is not uncommon for salespeople. However, too many of us stop there too often. Even good salespeople, after listening to the customer's problems, will jump in with something like this: "Okay, those sound like serious problems. Let me tell you how our solution can help." Again, the problem here is that research suggests that explaining the gap doesn't really affect performance or change. Upward counterfactual thinking does, though. So how can we get the buyer to focus on an upward counterfactual?

Instead of diving into an explanation of the benefits of your prod-uct or solution, help them imagine an upward counterfactual scenario by asking, "What if you had . . . ?" Here are three examples:

- "Thanks for sharing the challenges you're having with internal adoption of the current platform. What do you think would have happened with user adoption if you had implemented a system three years ago that had a better user interface?"
- "What would you have done with $20,000 if your current solu-tion had cost less?"
- "What would it be like today if your solution also had a dedi-cated customer service rep?"

---

9   "Counterfactual Thinking," ChangingMinds.org,
    http://changingminds.org/explanations/theories/counterfactual_thinking.htm.

COUNTERFACTUALS AND SPIN SELLING

This kind of rethinking of the past underscores why the questions in SPIN Selling can work so well. SPIN suggests you ask questions in the following stages: situation, problem, implications, and need-payoff. Upward counterfactuals relate directly to the implications and need-payoff phases of the SPIN methodology.

The key here is to avoid telling your prospect how your solution is superior and instead help them imagine how life could have been better today if they had implemented something different in the past. Research suggests this is more likely to cause them to change in the future (hopefully the near future).

TECHNOLOGY TIP

One way to help prospects imagine how life could have been better today is with a "vision demo." See Chapter 14 for more about different types of demos and the role technology plays in making them more effective.

You may not get the prospect's business right then, but by guiding them through upward counterfactual thinking, you are priming them to make a switch from your competition to you when the time is right.

Sales Skills That Support Buyer Enablement

Your role as an "enabler of buying" means that you have to be able to:

- Lead with strength and conviction
- Identify and connect with key decision makers

- Identify prospects' readiness to become buyers
- Sell the pain of change
- Map out the buying process
- Provoke a change in the buyer's mind

The more effective you are at these skills, the more effective each step of the buyer enablement framework will be.

PART II

DEEP-C™: A FRAMEWORK FOR IMPLEMENTING CUSTOMER FOCUS AND BUYER ENABLEMENT

DEEP-C: The 10,000-Foot View

As I discussed in the Introduction, companies that are easier to buy from have a strong competitive advantage. Sometimes it's easier to get in the buyer's mind by thinking about our own buying behavior and mentality as consumers. On a consumer level, two companies stand out that have capitalized on this: Apple and Amazon.

Apple did this incredibly well by streamlining the ability to buy songs and apps directly on the iPhone with one click. Amazon has made it easy to buy almost anything with one click. Both companies made it easier to buy and have become two of the most profitable companies in the world because of that.

Making buying easier is a more challenging process for B2B sales because so many stakeholders get involved. It takes a complete shift of mindset by salespeople, starting with the realization that they are not in charge of selling—their job shifts from "selling" to "helping customers buy."

The buyer enablement framework places the buying group at the gravitational center of the purchase and the champion at the core of that center. Behind it all, there is an assumption that facilitating and coaching the buying group is the only thing that can get the deal done; conversely, being unaware of needs somewhere in the buying group puts your deal at tremendous risk.

The skills needed to help customers buy focus on grooming and coaching champions so they can win over other stakeholders. The steps are likely different from what salespeople normally do, so I developed five principles that provide a guide to the kinds of actions they can take to connect with champions and other stakeholders:

- **D**iscover your champion and through them discover the other stakeholders.

- **E**ngage the champion and through them engage each stakeholder.

- **E**quip your internal champion with what they need to sell to the other stakeholders for you.

- **P**ersonalize value to each stakeholder.

- **C**oach the champion and other stakeholders through the buying process to a successful outcome.

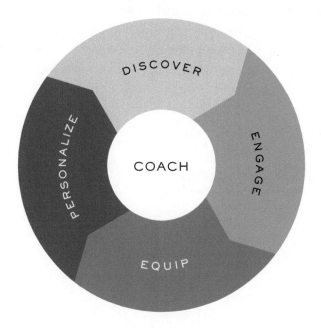

Figure 10: DEEP-C Buyer Enablement Framework.

This is what I call *DEEP-C Selling,* and it is especially useful when going after large, complex purchases that involve many stakeholders and decision makers.

The steps of the DEEP-C framework are only partially linear. Generally, you start by working with your initial point of contact until you discover and engage a champion (which may or may not be that initial contact), using information and tools personalized to their needs.

Coaching starts from the very beginning. As the sales representative for the solution you're selling, you are an expert not only in the buying process but also in how to help your champion solve their problems. Remember, though, that the best way to sell is to simply teach—or in other words, coach.

As the champion evolves into their selling role, you will operate in the role of a coach as you equip the champion with process steps, strategies, information, and tools to help them connect with and engage other stakeholders. You will help the champion know what to look out for and help them sell to the other stakeholders using information (demos, case studies, ROI calculations, etc.) personalized to those other stakeholders.

CHAPTER 6

DEEP-C: DISCOVER THE CHAMPION AND STAKEHOLDERS

"When all the details fit in perfectly, something
is probably wrong with the story."

—CHARLES BAXTER[1]

When I was a kid, we used to play this game called Pomp. We would get a group of ten or more friends together in somebody's yard. One of us would stand in the middle of the yard. The rest of the group would try to run to the other side without getting tackled by the person in the middle. If you were tackled, you joined the player in the middle, and as a group, you would try to tackle a couple more people the next time they raced across. The goal was to be the last man standing and make it across, weaving your way through the mob that was trying to bring you down.

Think of the champion as the first person you tackle. They join your team. Together you tackle the next few stakeholders. Once the

---

1   Charles Baxter, *Burning Down the House: Essays on Fiction* (Minneapolis: Graywolf Press, 2018): 26.

stakeholders are on board, it becomes easier to get the rest. But it all starts with the champion.

The "D" in DEEP-C stands for "discover"—meaning discovery of the champion and the stakeholders. It also means discovering what is driving their unique interests. Until you discover at least one true champion inside the target organization, you have no chance at getting traction with a deal. Until you discover the stakeholders and their unique interests, you have no chance at tailoring value to each stakeholder and closing the deal.

It's important to remember to look at things from your champions' perspective. They are trying to solve a problem. They don't start out thinking about you and your company. You reveal yourself to them and then become a partner in helping them solve their problem, and then they will become advocates and begin selling for you. Because they are trying to solve a problem in their own company, champions are going to try to sell for you no matter what you do. It's your role to find them before they begin selling so you can help them succeed.

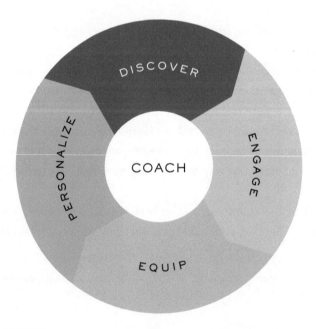

Figure 11: DISCOVER.

Establish Multiple Points of Contact

If you watch American football, you've seen the practice of "stripping the ball," a defensive tactic to try to force a fumble. The defensive player strikes the ball either upward or downward, hoping to dislodge it from the carrier's grasp. To prevent stripping, the best practice is to secure the football with six points of contact:

Figure 12: Six Points of Contact:[2] Think of holding on to your deal like holding on to a football. There are lots of forces trying to strip the ball away. Your six points of contact are the different stakeholders, who all need to be discovered, engaged, and bought in.

- 1st Point: Fingertips (Eagle Claw)
- 2nd Point: Palm
- 3rd Point: Forearm
- 4th Point: Bicep
- 5th Point: Chest
- 6th Point: The off hand will cover the top of the football, ensuring maximum ball security. This technique is used when the ball carrier encounters or anticipates a defender or defenders approaching to make a tackle.

Note that there are six points of contact used to secure the football. If a football player uses only some of the points of contact, the risk that they'll lose the ball increases. Think of the football as your buying

---

2   "How to Hold a Football," wikiHow, https://www.wikihow.com/Hold-a-Football.

group. If you want to hold on to a deal, you need multiple points of contact inside the target organization. According to Jill Konrath, author of four best-selling sales books, it's essential to establish relationships with all of the decision makers. "If you're only well connected to one or two people at a company, you're vulnerable if something happens to them."[3]

Anyone who is part of the buying group is a stakeholder, meaning they have skin in the game in terms of making the decision. Your goal is to find as many of these people as possible and turn one (and preferably more) of them into a champion, someone who will enthusiastically evangelize your solutions inside their company.

Leverage Your Contact to Reach Additional Stakeholders

You need to learn to discover, engage, and personalize your approach to every stakeholder in the buying group as early as possible to help neutralize group buying dysfunction. The way that most B2B salespeople discover the buying group today involves asking an initial point of contact who else needs to get involved. While this does yield some results, often that contact person doesn't really know—which means too often the stakeholders who really matter get involved late in the deal, massively increasing deal risk.

The buyer enablement way to accomplish the goal of reaching multiple stakeholders is:

- Make a map of the stakeholders who typically get involved (see the instructions later in this chapter or buyerenablement.io for a sample worksheet) and when (early, middle, late).

- Share that map with your contact person (who may be a potential champion) as early as possible in the sales process. Explain the reason for each stakeholder getting involved and what they are likely to care about.

---

3   Jill Konrath, "A Simple Strategy to Increase Win Rates," jillkonrath.com, blog, https://www.jillkonrath.com/using-linkedin-connections-to-expand-beyond-existing-contacts.

- Ask who the other stakeholders are who fit those roles, find out as much as you can about them, and encourage your contact to get any stakeholders involved who are needed at the current stage of the deal. You could say things such as this:
  - "We've seen the following roles need to get involved to get deals done in similar organizations. Who are these people inside your organization?"
  - "Who else do you think needs to get involved in this decision and why?"
  - "Who can block this purchase?"
  - "Who might have an interest in blocking this purchase and why?"

Jill Konrath also suggests that salespeople use the following kind of statements:

"Alex, I work with lots of other companies who are trying to decide if it makes good sense to change from the status quo. Virtually every time, the decision involves these types of people/ positions. Based on my experience, it's good to get them engaged as soon as possible."[4]

Note that she similarly recommends guiding the prospect to help you establish those stakeholder connections early and proactively, instead of waiting for the buying group to come together later. She also suggests following the initial recommendation with this: "I did some checking on LinkedIn, and this is my best guess who should be involved. Let's take a look at this list to see if it's right. And if not, determine who else we need to engage."[5]

Take a look at the tone here. She's not recommending the rep say, "So, if you think it's a good idea, what do you think about . . ." Instead, there is a tone of leadership and expertise: "Let's take a look at this list . . ."

---

4   Konrath, "A Simple Strategy to Increase Win Rates."
5   Konrath, "A Simple Strategy to Increase Win Rates."

BE WILLING TO STAND YOUR GROUND

Be willing to go so far as to say something like, "I really can't get this deal done on our side until we get those stakeholders involved. In our experience, deals that don't have these roles represented in the buying group end up not implementing very effectively and are at high risk for not realizing the value that we can provide. We want you as a customer for years, not just to get this one deal done."

This can feel painful if you're not used to it, but it establishes leadership and confidence, and if practiced early in the process, it will actually shorten your sales cycle. Just remember, you're guiding them through assembling the group that would eventually form anyway. You're just doing it earlier and in a planned way.

Map the Buying Group: Personas vs. People

You've been through the selling and buying process associated with your company's products multiple times. So you know *typically* what kinds of people (meaning their job title or responsibilities) need to be involved in order for the decision to be made quickly (and in your favor). You can use this knowledge to help educate your buyers by mapping out the types of people who possibly need to be involved and their main interests.

I call a specific kind of decision maker a persona, or a person or group of people who behave in similar ways. They often have similar goals or objectives. They often have similar concerns or objections to your product or solution. They don't always share the same title but are often overseeing the same function.

For example, you might know that a financial persona should be involved in the purchase decision, someone concerned with the cost of the investment and the kind of return expected. In one customer organization, the title of the person concerned with the financial aspects might be the VP of finance, but in another it might be the CFO, and in yet another the controller. No matter what the job title is, the bottom line is that in order for the purchase decision to be concluded successfully, there must be a person overseeing the financial part of the deal who is part of the buying group.

In your role as coach of your champion, you can help them understand the buying process by sketching out the kinds of personas who should be involved. There are some tips in Figure 13.

GUIDELINES FOR PERSONA DEVELOPMENT

A GOOD PERSONA IS...	A GOOD PERSONA ISN'T...
▪ Prioritized information about what is important to the role ▪ Contextualized to the enterprise buying process and team ▪ Fact-based (includes the voice of the role) ▪ A living document	▪ A laundry list of every available fact about the role ▪ Solely concerned with the individual buyer ▪ Purely anecdotal ▪ Done just once

© 2018 Gartner, Inc.

Figure 13: In my opinion this Gartner graphic is a short but good summary of how to define a persona. Don't take the exercise to an extreme.

According to Gartner:

Persona development, when done well, can be a powerful tool, both to develop this organizational understanding of these new buyers and to engage with them effectively. But it must be grounded in research that starts with learning what is important to the buyer, not starting from "how we are relevant to the buyer."[6]

---

6   Gartner, *Construct B2B Personas to Improve Demand Generation*, Noah Elkin, January 14, 2020.

Start by getting a team together, including the people on your sales team who have been around the longest (and have won and lost the most deals) and those who are able to adapt to the needs of different buyer personas. Work with them to write up descriptions of the personas and identify when each should be involved in the buying process.

As you do the analysis, consider the different levels of authority or power that the personas typically have regarding the decision. Often their lens is based on the role they play in the purchasing decision. I like the way that *Inc.* described the three roles:

1. The Access Owner helps you connect with other stakeholders.

2. The Problem Owner is the stakeholder who owns the problem your product or solution addresses.

3. The Budget Owner is, of course, the person who has control of the money needed to implement the solution the Problem Owner needs to implement.[7]

Based on my own experience, I'd add another role: those with veto power. My sales team often encounters situations where the IT group has the ability to say no even though they are not users of our product. Being clear about who has what kind of authority regarding the decision is another critical aspect of developing sound strategies for closing a sale.

If you go through this kind of exercise with your team, you'll be surprised at how much collective information you have across your team about your buyers and personas without having to do lots of additional research. (You can always add descriptions to the personas as you learn from each new client.)

You should then create a list or map of these personas, documented in a way that you can share with the champion. As noted earlier, you will be asking the champion to help you put the names of people next to each persona.

---

7   Geoffrey James, "Sales Tip: Know All 3 Decision Makers," *Inc.*,
     https://www.inc.com/geoffrey-james/sales-tip-know-all-3-decision-makers.html.

The following table shows an example from my own company. In one type of sale, there are six types of personas that need to get involved in order for a deal to close. The labels for those personas are listed in the first column; the sales rep would enter the names of the person or people who fill those personas in the right column. In this example, the rep has one unidentified persona, and filling in that name will be critical for the deal to move forward. An initial buying group map could be as simple as something like this:

TABLE B

Persona	Person
Sales Leader	Oliver
End User Manager	Kristin
IT InfoSec	Todd
C-Level Exec	Diego
Finance	Jerome
Marketing Leader	???

Use Technology to Speed Up Stakeholder Discovery

Under the old (and current, for many reps) methods of selling, the only way to discover and engage champions and stakeholders was to wait for a first appointment, ask a lot of questions, work your way slowly through the organization chart, and eventually find someone who was willing to be an ally.

To close B2B sales faster, we need to discover and engage the buying group more quickly. To do this, create and send sales content to your point of contact (or the key sponsor or champion, if you know who they are already). They will naturally share the information with other stakeholders in their buying group.

If you do this using buyer enablement technology, you can create intraviral content, meaning the content you send to a contact or champion can quickly spread inside their organization. Further, the technology should allow you to track who is looking at this content—that's one way you can discover who else is going to be involved in the decision process.

We don't care if the person we send the content to shares it with their grandma (that's for cute cat videos), but we *do* care and want to know whether they share it with their CEO, their VP of marketing, and so on—whoever the key stakeholders are in the buying group. It's not enough to just send out links to our contacts; we need to know who else sees the content we provide and whether those people engage with it.

WHEN TO USE INTRAVIRAL CONTENT FOR STAKEHOLDER DISCOVERY

You should use intraviral content at many different stages of the sales funnel, including right at the top of the funnel. What we've found studying our own account development data is that if a prospect engages with an interactive video demo and shares it with at least one other person before engaging with the account executive, they are 81% more likely to become a qualified opportunity.[8]

A Case Study in Intraviral Discovery

As an example, I recently had a key champion inside Oracle, an important prospect account, email me a question about a feature of the Consensus analytics. I launched the screen recorder and created a quick unscripted video demo that answered his questions, and I sent it back to him just a few minutes later. He instantly shared it with four

---

8   Consensus Sales, Inc., 2016 Account Development Gap Study.

people on his team. They, in turn, after viewing it, began sharing it with others, and in the end, it was shared with 11 different stakeholders, some in the current buying group and others in other areas of the organization. 8 of the 11 watched some or all of the rapid video demo that took me only a few minutes to create. Presto! I quickly had the names of 11 more people who were interested in the buying decision, 8 of whom were interested enough to engage with the content. (See more on engaging stakeholders in the next chapter.)

Figure 14 is a view of the Buying Group Dashboard showing everyone the video was shared with (with names blurred, of course).

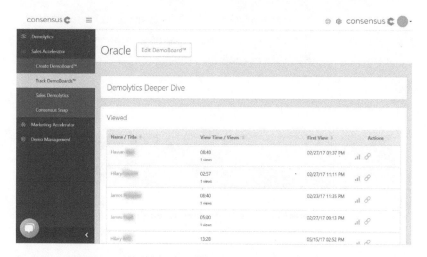

Figure 14: Buying Group Dashboard: Collectively, this buying group watched 76 minutes of video content, and more importantly, Consensus was spontaneously introduced to ten additional stakeholders related to the current deal or expansion opportunities.

2 minutes to send, 10 stakeholders discovered, 76 minutes of video engagement.

This technology that helps you discover stakeholders can also be used to engage them more effectively by personalizing the content.

TECHNOLOGY TIP

The example I've shared is with interactive video demos, but you can get some of the same benefits with documents too. Do you have HubSpot? If you do, turn on the "Require email address to view document" setting so that when documents shared through HubSpot get shared, you can start to track who is engaging. These are most likely people who are interested in the purchase either because they will be affected by the outcome and/or have a say in the decision–(i.e., your stakeholders).

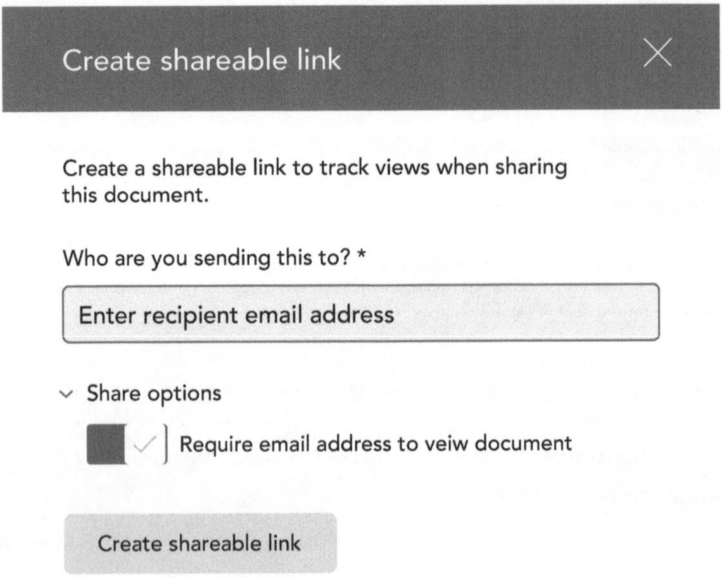

Create shareable link   ✕

Create a shareable link to track views when sharing this document.

Who are you sending this to? *

Enter recipient email address

∨ Share options

☑ | Require email address to veiw document

Create shareable link

Figure 15.

Is Your Contact a True Champion?

How can you tell which of the contacts inside your organization is a champion?

You'll know you have your champion if they:

- Are passionate about solving the key problem your solution addresses

- Begin advocating before you begin asking them about promoting the solution

- Begin sharing content that you send them with other peers and colleagues who are potentially in the buying group

- Have influence and political credibility to influence or make the decision

- Are willing to make the emotional investment necessary to advocate for change inside their organization

- Are willing to take on the risks inherent in championing a change that is not guaranteed to succeed

- Have a personal stake in the outcome (such as advancing their careers)

Equally important to anything on that list is this: A true champion will make and keep commitments that move the buying process forward.

If Your Contact Wants to Be Your Champion but Isn't One

Your first contact often becomes your champion, but be aware that they may not be the right person to get the decision made and the deal done. Beware of the following signs that you don't really have a champion, even though your prospect might say they want to lead the charge:

- They are willing to meet with you week after week but never take the risks needed to advocate for your solution. This could take the form of endless delays before they will take the proposed solution to their boss.
- They can't seem to coherently speak about your message.
- They lack political influence or sufficient rank inside the organization. (This is not necessarily a knockout factor: Even lower-level professionals can become great champions and will often see the opportunity as a way to further their careers.)

TECHNOLOGY TIP

Make sure to use a digital content technology that encourages sharing and tracks who the links are shared with. If a contact begins sharing your content with other stakeholders, that is usually a sign they are beginning to advocate, and they could be your champion.

It takes courage; an ability to build consensus by working through differing interests, opinions, and concerns; and an unyielding desire to effect change to be an effective B2B buying champion. If you discover that your contact talks and talks about effecting change but isn't doing the things necessary to move the deal forward, follow the steps in the next section about discovering additional stakeholders. If you make contact with someone who seems enthusiastic about your solution, ask them these questions:

- "Would you be willing to take the lead in heading up this change inside your organization?"
- "You seem to be someone who could really have an impact for good on your organization by helping to bring this solution to

life. Would you be willing to take this on and drive the consensus required to achieve these results?"

Once you get a commitment from your new champion, begin leading and coaching them as described in the section on coaching your champions.

When You *Thought* You Had the Decision Maker

Have you ever asked, or seen someone on your team ask, the prospect, "Are you the decision maker?" and you get a "Yes, I can make the final decision on this purchase" only to hear the prospect say, on the day you're expecting a signature, "Oh, yeah, we'll get this signed just as soon as I can get this in front of my boss"? This example underscores both the lack of buying experience the buyer has (it's not their fault) and the risk that unknown stakeholders pose to B2B sales.

Stakeholders who are unknown to you represent arguably the largest risk to your deal because they can appear at any time and deep-six your deal without warning. Some salespeople prefer to try to prevent the buying group from getting large in the hopes they can sneak one through. While this may prove successful every now and then, it usually positions the deal for late-stage risk and decreases the likelihood the deal will get done.

The reality is that multiple stakeholders must get involved for the process to end in a purchase that works for the buyer. As an experienced sales rep, you've seen companies go through the purchasing process dozens of times, maybe more. You know from experience which people likely don't have the clout and impact to be an important decision maker but still go along if they say they are the decision maker. Then when the deal falls through or stalls, you say to yourself, "Oh, I thought this might happen!"

If your experience tells you that the so-called decision maker is not the decision maker, follow up with a question such as "I can appreciate that you say you're the decision maker, but when working with other companies like yours, I've found that there is often another role that has to get involved. Before we can really move forward, we need to verify with that person that they do not need to get involved in the purchase. Would you be willing to double-check to make sure that you have the final say?"

Competing Champions

While we're on the topic of discovering a champion, it's worth pointing out that there might be more than one champion. Often there is a lower-level champion who promotes your solution internally and eventually converts their boss into a higher-level champion. This may continue up the chain if the deal crosses division boundaries. This can be great, but as deals go across divisions in large companies, you may run into additional champions who share an interest in solving the problem but aren't necessarily all championing the *same* solution. Paul Norris shares this cautionary tale that shows the perspective from the standpoint of the buyer:

> At AIG we were buying software for cloud deployment. The company already had a huge number of vendors already providing services, so even though there was going to be a primary buyer, there were a lot of supporting groups as stakeholders.
>
> In this case, the buyer with the architecture team I was on preferred CA Technologies, but the engineering team preferred IBM. IBM ended up winning because the CTO liked working with IBM and had good relationships.
>
> So you can do all of the work and enable your champions only to be overridden because of previous relationships.[9]

---

9   Paul Norris, in discussion with the author, January 26, 2018.

This scenario happens frequently when there is an initiative to roll up otherwise disparate pockets of technology that are solving similar problems into one global solution or standard.

If you find yourself in this situation, you need to do two things:

1. Double down on enabling the champion(s) whom you do have. "The champion that is best enabled will have a better chance of selling internally," says Paul. Think of it as a competition between internal champions. The ones who are better equipped will be more effective at driving interest and consensus inside their organization.

2. Raise your sights and recognize that the buying group might expand well outside your current sphere of influence. You may need to involve higher-level stakeholders from your own organization to help build and drive relationships with higher-level contacts in the target company. Remember, the goal is to discover and build a relationship with the champion at whatever level is going to get the job done for you.

Alternatively, you might have two champions in different divisions, or inside the same division, who want to take the credit for bringing your solution to their organization. Instead of getting the deal done, they engage in endless positioning, hoping to secure the credit before they will do the deal. As I'm writing this book, we are in the midst of this very problem in a deal we are pursuing at my company.

One champion is good. More than one often leads to more challenges. If possible, try to get an entry deal done with the first champion before engaging other champions, whose additional enthusiasm and personal interests could threaten your deal.

Sometimes You Need to Give Up

What??? Did I just say, "Give up"? I know what you're thinking: *I was told never to give up.* Let me explain.

Years ago, at age 19, I was walking the streets of Cordoba, Argentina, as a young missionary for my church. (I'm a devout member of the Church of Jesus Christ of Latter-day Saints, sometimes known, inaccurately, as Mormons—and no, this isn't a plug for religion, so keep reading.) What does that have to do with sales? Well, without realizing it, on those hot, dusty streets, I was getting my first lessons in effective selling. After weeks of getting mostly "No, sorry, boys, we're not interested" as a response to our efforts, the sting of rejection was expected but still painful. Consequently, sometimes we would also engage in long conversations with people. However, some of these folks really weren't interested and likely would never be interested in what we had to say. I wondered if I would ever get over the daily feeling of failure.

Months later, my perspective changed. Instead of feeling the pang of disappointment, I had learned to feel positively when people told us they weren't interested. Why? Because I had come to realize that getting the no responses behind me as quickly as possible would give me more time to find someone who was interested and say yes. I've now been involved in B2B sales for more than 15 years, and I've relearned the same lesson: We usually don't give up soon enough.

We often get so enamored with a specific deal that over time our blinders go on. "It would be such a great deal!" we tell ourselves. We spend more and more time working with the prospect and even begin ignoring small signs that there could be problems, because we want it so badly. The customer starts delaying. The decision-making process gets overly complicated. The buyer is totally on board, and then they start looking at competitors' solutions. You know the kind of deal I'm talking about.

So what do we do? Too often, we persist. "Never, never, never give up" goes the common adage. Well, that's good advice if someone is bombing your homeland, but that's flawed thinking in sales. In sales, we need to give up as quickly as it makes sense. Why? Because even though it feels like failure, in reality, every minute of time and every ounce of energy we spend on a prospect who isn't interested is time and energy we could be spending on a prospect who truly is a great candidate. Think of the opportunity cost.

The real question is this: If I weren't spending time on this client, what other buying groups could I be working with that are willing to commit? Let's take a look at the cost. Suppose you lead a team of ten reps. What if each rep on the team is spending just four hours a week with prospects who aren't ready? That's 40 hours a month that could be used to close other better-qualified prospects.

In sales leadership, it's imperative to develop a team habit of not only excellent lead qualification but also rapid prospect disqualification once those leads are in the pipeline. The sooner you get to a "no" or "not now" or recognize a legitimate stall, the sooner you'll be spending more of your time with people who say yes. The bottom line is that if you don't have a champion who is willing to fight for the cause inside their organization, you need to either:

- give up on that champion and search for another, or
- give up on the entire organization for the time being in favor of other organizations who are ready and willing to take the risks necessary to effect change.

You can find out if you have a champion by asking them to commit to certain tasks that will move the decision-making process forward. If they commit, see if they follow through. If they do, they are likely your champion. If they don't, try one more time to recommit them, and if they don't follow through again, drop them.

And when I say drop them, don't drop them permanently; just put them in a long-term nurturing campaign, but stop wasting your valuable time so that you can spend it with champions on teams that will commit. If they aren't willing to go to bat for the strategic advantage your solution offers, either the timing isn't ready or they will never be your champion.

Everything Begins with Discovery

One of the most common pitfalls in traditional selling is when a stakeholder unknown to the sales rep enters the buying process late or works behind the scenes to sabotage a deal. If the sales rep doesn't know who all the key stakeholders are, they've lost the deal. If they don't know which stakeholder will work as their internal champion, they've lost the deal.

That's why I put discovery at the front of DEEP-C. It's an activity you should start immediately and continue throughout your customer's buying process to increase the odds that you will know who all the important players are. The discovery process will go much, much faster if buyer enablement technology is involved, but either way, discovery is critical to improving your odds of closing a deal.

CHAPTER 7

DEEP-C: ENGAGE EACH STAKEHOLDER

"In motivating people, you've got to engage their minds and their hearts."
—RUPERT MURDOCH

Let's start with some buyer empathy. None of our prospects wake up thinking about us; they wake up thinking about themselves. Each stakeholder who gets involved in the purchasing process is already doing something else. They have a long list of projects and tasks they are accountable for. The purchase that you want them to complete is simply one of many issues on their plates.

To get the attention of a stakeholder, you must engage with them about the problems *they* are trying to solve. The best way to do that is to provide them with information that is more compelling than whatever is already drawing their attention and focus—information that makes it clear what the risks are if they don't take action, the benefits if they do, and the ROI of making a change. If you can't grab their attention, the buying process will never get anywhere.

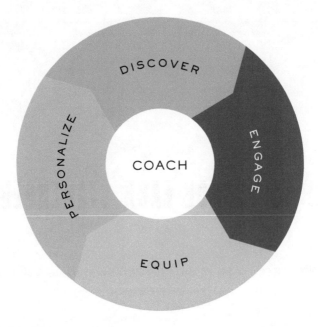

Figure 16: ENGAGE.

Positive and Negative Reasons Stakeholders Engage

You will encounter some stakeholders who will engage with you and the process for positive reasons (meaning they support your solution) and some who will engage for negative reasons. Some of the positive reasons stakeholders engage are:

- Their boss asks them to.
- A colleague they trust invites them to engage.
- They possess inherent self-interest to solve a problem they need to solve.
- They possess inherent self-interest to advance their careers.
- The content is intriguing.

Any of these are reasons for initial engagement, but to keep stakeholders engaged throughout the deal, you ultimately need to build a relationship with each of them. Each stakeholder perceives value differently. You need to learn what is driving their unique interests and tailor your messaging to the way they perceive value.

In contrast, some stakeholders may also engage for various negative reasons:

- They perceive the change your champion is attempting as a threat to their department's objectives or the overall success of the company.

- They perceive your champion's cause as a personal threat to their individual success.

- They may see an opportunity to do damage to a political opponent inside the organization.

If a stakeholder is engaged for negative reasons, they become a threat to your champion's effort to effect change in the organization and the buying journey. When that happens, you and your champion need to work at neutralizing their influence by attempting one of the following strategies:

- Seek to truly understand their objections. Educate them on why the risks of implementing your solution are outweighed by the value for their department or organization.

- Engage the stakeholder personally and gain their trust through relationship building.

- Engage stakeholders with more authority or political influence who can counter the detractor's influence in the buying group.

- Find ways to remove them from the buying group by reducing the solution's scope of impact in a way that won't affect their domain.

- Get creative and find ways to remove them from the buying group using other means.

So often we think the sale is in the hands of the customer. Of course they have the ultimate say, as they are the ones doing the purchasing. But we often underestimate our potential for dramatically influencing the sale. You won't believe what one salesperson did to win the biggest sale of his career. Keep in mind that this story may seem extreme, but I want you to focus on the attitude of the salesperson and their effort at creativity in solving the problem.

This story was told to me by Adam Slovik, a partner at Select Venture Partners, one of our investors at Consensus. Adam was an early employee at one of the largest software companies in the world when it was a young startup in hyper-growth mode, competing with much bigger players. The sale was in the tens of millions of dollars to a large university in the United States. There were three decision makers. They had agreed that because the decision would impact every member of staff at the university, they would need to have unanimous consensus to make a final decision.

Two of the three wanted to do the deal. But the last one not only didn't prefer their company but also wanted anything *but* their company. She was a big-time blocker. After several attempts to win her over, the salesperson knew they would not be able to close this deal with her on that buying panel. Most salespeople would eventually move on, considering this an impasse. Not this guy.

This salesperson called a recruiter and paid their fees to have them try to recruit this person away from the university to a better position. The recruiter succeeded, and the third member of the buying panel left the university for another job. They replaced her with someone else, whom they were able to win to their side, and the salesperson closed the deal.

That is avoiding the victim mentality and taking control of the sale, if I've ever heard of it. Most of us won't be able to pull off that kind of feat, but there is usually more that we can do to influence the purchasing decision than we want to admit. It's often the hard, difficult, perhaps not repeatable thing that can make the difference. When the deal is worth it, do whatever it takes to gain maximum influence in the purchasing decision.

What Should We Engage Stakeholders About?

The buying group has to come to agreement in one form or another on all of the different questions of the purchasing cycle. What should we engage them about? The buying process. Effectively, the questions they need answers to:

- Is there a problem?
- Should we solve it?
- Should we solve it now?
- How should we solve it?
- Which is the right vendor to work with?
- What are the risks? Is there proof they've solved this before?
- Is this financially feasible, and how do we measure the return on our investment?
- How do we implement this effectively to ensure success?

There is a lot written about the buying process from many different angles. If you do a Google search for "B2B buying process," you'll find varying opinions about what the buying process is. I really like Kevin Davis's six-stage buying-process model (plus two extra steps post-sale):

1. Change: becomes aware of a potential issue and receptive to alternatives and remedies

2. Discontent: conducts problem analysis and economic analysis, develops "solution vision"

3. Research: learns from supplier(s) how vision could be implemented, defines formal and informal decision criteria, prepares a formal or informal RFP

4. Comparison: establishes short list, analyzes proposals, attends demos

5. Fear: tests Proof of Concept (POC), checks references

6. Commitment: negotiates terms and conditions[1]

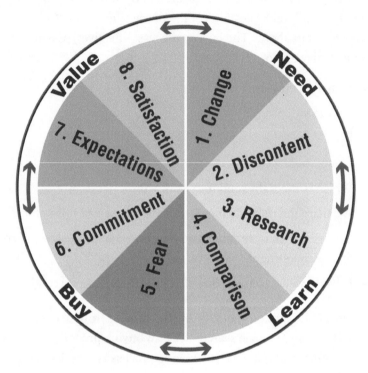

Figure 17: Kevin Davis's Buying Model.

This model, as buyer-centric as it is, is written from the perspective of a seller observing the buyer process. For example, "fear" as a stage in the process is not a term a buyer would likely use to describe their journey.

Interestingly, Gartner describes the buying process as having six parts as well. "Virtually every B2B purchase spans six distinct 'jobs' that buyers must complete to their satisfaction to successfully complete a complex purchase: Problem identification, Solution exploration, Requirements building, Supplier selection, Validation, Consensus

1   Kevin F. Davis, *The Sales Manager's Guide to Greatness: 10 Essential Strategies for Leading Your Team to the Top* (Austin: Greenleaf Book Group, 2017): 95.

creation." Further, "although these six jobs occur in each interaction, the way in which customers progress from the starting point to a purchase is unpredictable, inconsistent and sometimes repetitive."

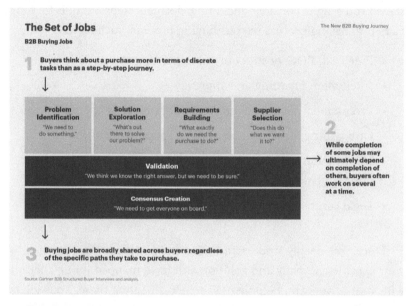

Figure 18: Gartner's "The Set of Jobs."[2]

In some sense, all of the steps are recursive because as new stakeholders join the buying group, they often bring new insights and perspectives that require the champion and the group to redefine or update each job to be more complete. In short, none of these jobs are complete until they are validated and consensus is achieved across the group.

Both of these models are very useful, but they are general models, and what your buyers need is a process that is specific to your industry, product, and organization, including steps to be taken at each general stage. So whether you start with Davis's model or Gartner's model or one of your own, what you need to do is map out a specific buying process that you can share with your buyer and that they can engage with

2   Gartner, *Win More B2B Sales Deals*, Brent Adamson, 2018.

as an accurate representation of what they will need to go through to make a purchasing decision. This may vary based on industry, size, and other segmentation criteria.

Now add tasks that the buying group needs to complete at each stage. You might consider including detailed steps unique to your SaaS purchasing process in your buying process, such as:

- Free trial, POC, or Proof of Value (POV)
- Integration planning and approval
- Professional services planning and approval (if applicable)
- Onboarding, implementation, and adoption planning
- Information security (InfoSec) and GDPR (general data protection regulation) approval
- Legal contract review

Once you deeply understand the buying process that applies to your specific company and solution and have mapped it out, share it with your buyers and help them see the path before them. Your job is to confidently and tactfully ask them to commit to each stage in the process as they progress.

As they commit, also make a plan to engage each stakeholder (as needed) at each stage. Quite often, the deals that don't make it fall through because some influencer in the deal doesn't get brought along with everyone else. This causes friction that leads to the deal falling apart.

Use LinkedIn to Assist in Stakeholder Engagement

Once you have mapped out your typical buying group personas and collaborated with your champion to detail the exact people you should be engaging, consider using LinkedIn to reach out proactively to them with or without an introduction from your champion.

Here's my recommendation on the verbiage to use when making the connection request or sending an InMail outreach:

Hi [first name],

I've been working with [champion full name] over in [department or division name] to help [company name] with [value prop].

In my experience, when working with companies like yours, it's important to get someone in your role involved when making this decision. Could we schedule a brief call so I can explain what we're trying to accomplish, get your input, and answer any questions you might have?

I look forward to meeting with you.

[your name]

Here's how this template might look filled out:

Hi Janet,

I've been working with Jake Thompson over in the Tronix Product Security Department to help MetaCortex improve data security policy communication and compliance.

In my experience, when working with companies like yours, it's important to get someone in your role involved. Could we schedule a brief call so I can explain what we're trying to accomplish, get your input, and answer any questions you might have?

I look forward to meeting with you.

Garin

Learn Stakeholder Interests and Objectives

Some artists use perspective with the same sculpture to portray something completely different. Figure 19 shows two views of the same sculpture by French artist Matthieu Robert-Ortis. In the view from the left (taken from the front), it appears to be two giraffes. When you walk around to view it from the side, you see something completely different (photo on the right).

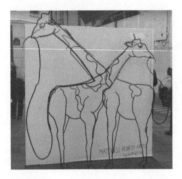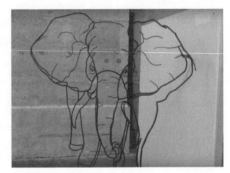

Figure 19: The Same Sculpture from Two Views: Is this sculpture an elephant or a pair of giraffes? It is both, of course. And that's how the purchase of your solution looks to different stakeholders and why the same deal at the same company can cause confusion and misunderstanding.

Artists call this anamorphosis. If you are intrigued by this phenomenon, check out artist Michael Murphy or watch online an Apple commercial that uses anamorphosis.[3]

The problem your champion is trying to solve and the solution you and the champion bring to the table are like these sculptures—viewing the problem and solution from different angles brings a completely different perspective. Each stakeholder is viewing the problem and solution in a completely different way, based on their unique needs and experiences.

Here, the connections between the DEEP-C steps are the most

---

3 "Apple-Perspective," Apple, YouTube, September 9, 2014,
   https://www.youtube.com/watch?v=TJ1SDXbij8Y&app=desktop.

obvious. One of the reasons for engaging different stakeholders is so that you can get a full picture of their interests, objectives, and needs. Once you know their interests and objectives, you can personalize (the "P" of DEEP-C) your messaging and solution education to them.

How Technology Can Help You Learn Stakeholders' Unique Interests

Technology that supports buyer enablement will automate some of the discovery process, especially if it relies on content with the potential to go intraviral after being shared by your champion. If structured correctly, the technology can help you capture what it is that each person is most interested in.

As an example, when the champion shares an automated demo through the Consensus software platform, the automated demo first asks questions of each stakeholder who engages with the video demo (see Figure 21) so that it can know how to tailor the demo to their unique interests.

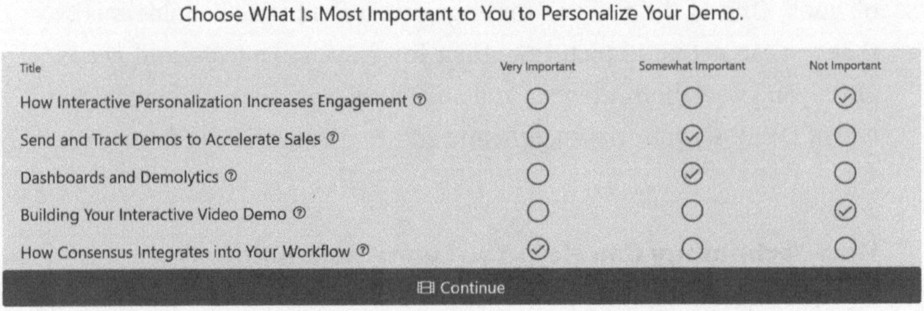

Choose What Is Most Important to You to Personalize Your Demo.

Title	Very Important	Somewhat Important	Not Important
How Interactive Personalization Increases Engagement ⑦	○	○	✓
Send and Track Demos to Accelerate Sales ⑦	○	✓	○
Dashboards and Demolytics ⑦	○	✓	○
Building Your Interactive Video Demo ⑦	○	○	✓
How Consensus Integrates into Your Workflow ⑦	✓	○	○

⊞ Continue

Figure 21: Personalization Screen: Like an effective salesperson, this buyer enablement technology first asks the buyer to rate the importance level before deciding what content to provide. What is delivered to each person will depend on their ratings.

The software then curates different video clips and documents to provide an interactive demo experience that is more relevant to them. It tracks and displays a map of the different responses so you and your champion can see where there is alignment or misalignment across different stakeholders.[4]

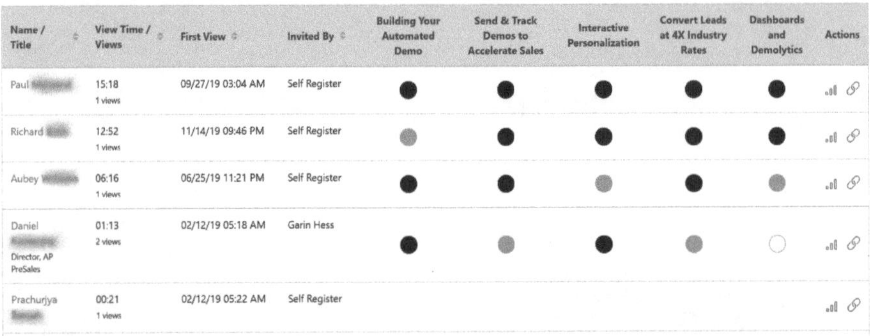

Name / Title	View Time / Views	First View	Invited By	Building Your Automated Demo	Send & Track Demos to Accelerate Sales	Interactive Personalization	Convert Leads at 4X Industry Rates	Dashboards and Demolytics	Actions
Paul	15:18 / 1 views	09/27/19 03:04 AM	Self Register	●	●	●	●	●	.ıl 🔗
Richard	12:52 / 1 views	11/14/19 09:46 PM	Self Register	◐	●	●	●	●	.ıl 🔗
Aubey	06:16 / 1 views	06/25/19 11:21 PM	Self Register	●	●	◐	●	◐	.ıl 🔗
Daniel Director, AP PreSales	01:13 / 2 views	02/12/19 05:18 AM	Garin Hess	◐	◐	●	◐	○	.ıl 🔗
Prachurjya	00:21 / 1 views	02/12/19 05:22 AM	Self Register						.ıl 🔗

Figure 22: Comparison of Stakeholder Interests: Some technology can help you see where there are misalignments or gaps in buying group alignment. In this view you can visually see where interests are similarly high or nonexistent.

One sales leader said this approach is "like having the answers before the test" because this data helped them set up the live conversation

4   Consensus Sales, Inc. www.goconsensus.com

more effectively. By sending out an automated demo ahead of a conversation with a stakeholder, you may learn things about their unique interests to help you build the relationship and understand how stakeholders are perceiving the opportunity and risks associated with the changes your champion is advocating.

Four Sales Skills That Drive Engagement

As they begin working with your initial contact, champion, and other stakeholders, there are four sales skills that reps will find most useful:

1. Punch their pain

2. Create urgency

3. Clearly explain the advantages of your solution over the competition

4. Preemptively address common objections

Punch Their Pain

One of the best ways to help increase the desire to solve the problem is to exacerbate the pain. In other words, if you want someone to see the need for pain relief, they need to be focused on the pain. When people experience pain of a current problem or the fear of missing out on an opportunity, you increase their desire to take action.

Though it seems a bit graphic, the image of punching someone's wounded shoulder evokes a strong emotion. The reason we have to punch their pain is because they've become so used to living with it they have almost forgotten it is there.

One sales leader I have worked with calls it "dragging your buyer through the glass." Again, a startling violent image, but it's meant to remind us that without helping the buyers fully comprehend the pain of their current situation, they usually won't feel motivated enough to take action.

I have an uncle who for years was warned by the doctor to lose some weight, start exercising, and get in better health. My uncle never did take action and died at a relatively young age from heart disease, which was probably preventable. The reason? My uncle didn't experience much pain or discomfort until the day his heart failed. It was some but not enough. The fault lies primarily with my uncle, but I'll place some of the fault at the doctor's feet too. In my opinion, doctors need to show some graphic images or show some video testimonials of people whose loved ones died early and left them bereft. Why? It is painting the picture of inaction.

Our prospects are often like my uncle, sometimes knowing they have a problem but not experiencing enough pain to take action. This can take the form of inefficient processes or just not seeing an opportunity that could change their outcomes in a major way. Our prospects all get comfortable with their current situation, and it is our job to make them uncomfortable. Our job, as guides in the buyer journey, is to increase their discomfort to the point they believe they need to act.

So your content needs to find the pain and punch it. Then punch it again. This will get each stakeholder to sit up and pay attention. Your human reps might feel a little uncomfortable doing this, and that's okay (and remember, your digital content needn't be squeamish). Remember that the goal here is to get the buying group to take action that will help them in a big way. Without the focus on the pain, your prospects aren't motivated to take action, your sales cycles stretch out, and you'll lose deals that otherwise you should be closing.

Create Urgency

Once you have educated the champion and other stakeholders on why they need to solve the problem, focus on educating them on why they should solve it now. Some stakeholders (especially the champion) feel a deep sense of urgency to solve the problem they are tackling and to tackle it as quickly as possible. Other stakeholders may not. So part of your stakeholder education needs to involve cost of delay, inaction, and missed opportunities. Without creating this sense of urgency, stakeholders may not get as deeply involved as they need to, causing unnecessary delays in getting the purchase done.

Note that educating the stakeholders on the cost of delay and inaction doesn't necessarily mean you are promoting your own company yet. You first need to help them recognize they need to solve the problem right now. That said, the added benefit of helping customers understand the problem and educating them on potential solutions means that they are likely to look to you as one of the specific sources of help when trying to solve the problem.

Clearly Explain the Advantages of Your Solution over the Competition

Once a company decides to solve the problem, they must select a specific vendor to help them solve that problem. One of the keys is helping the stakeholders understand the difference between your offering and other offerings. By being transparent about how other vendors can help but positioning yourself in a way to help in a unique way, you increase trust and help the stakeholders make sense of the competitive landscape.

In this process, never disparage another vendor. In fact, compliment them on things they do well that are of relatively little importance to your prospect. Be sincere about it. We all have envy toward other vendors and things they do better than we do. But the key is to make certain that our sincere compliments point out differentiations that are largely meaningless to solving the main problem the customer has. For example, when it comes to demo automation in presales, at Consensus we might tell our customers:

Sometimes our prospects look at general video-streaming platforms such as Wistia as a potential solution. They are a great platform for managing videos and are an excellent choice for single videos used in marketing for lead gen. But we're not talking about lead gen here. What we're talking about is scaling the sales-engineering function.

What Consensus does is quite different from Wistia. Consensus asks questions of the viewer that lead to personalized content and then tracks those questions and engagement across the buying group. This allows you to automate early requests for demos so you can better qualify prospects before assigning expensive and scarce sales-engineering resources to the account.

Do you see how complimenting Wistia on something they do well doesn't take anything away from what Consensus does well? Yet we also make the point that what *we* do well is more directly linked to this customer's priority needs than what Wistia does.

What would that look like for your company? Make a list of direct competitors and those in tangential markets that sometimes leak into your sales conversations, and then list some of their best features that solve problems that your target market is not trying to solve. When you're done, educate your champion on how to educate the other stakeholders on this. Provide them with supporting materials to help them when the question invariably comes up, "Hey, I know you're talking to [your company], but I also heard of [your competition], and they might be someone to look into."

TECHNOLOGY TIP

Where possible, look for buyer enablement sharing platforms that recommend content by role or segment automatically. Technology should allow you to tag the content in a way that the combination of title personas, industry, and company size and use case combine to automatically recommend key resources for the champion to use when approaching different stakeholders.

Preemptively Address Common Objections

Along the way, your prospects will have concerns.

The 2017 Gartner Technology Buying Dynamics Survey provides, "Surveyed buyers report that 'cost' is the No. 1 most frequent objection internally to purchase decisions. 'Risk' follows as the No. 2 most frequently cited objection, and both are cited as the two most time-consuming objections to resolve."[5]

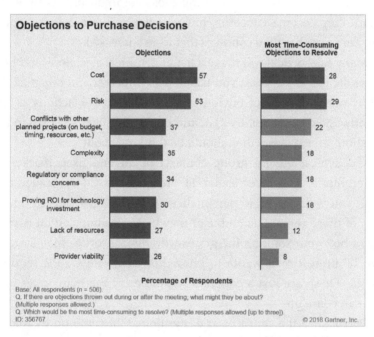

Figure 23: Gartner's "Objections to Purchase Decisions": Research from Gartner shows objections thrown out during or after the meeting and the most time-consuming objections to resolve. We encourage you to make your own list and then decide when you proactively bring them up.[6]

As a trusted partner and guide through the buying journey, instead of trying to sweep the risks under the carpet, you should bring them

---

5   Gartner, *Tech Go-to-Market: Use Business Outcome Messaging to Attract Attention and Engagement from New Prospects*, Michele Buckley, Chrissy Healey, December 11, 2018.

6   Gartner, Tech Go-to-Market: Why Tech Sales Cycles Are Taking So Long and What Needs to Be Done Now, Michele Buckley, June 4, 2018.

out in the open before they ever come up, but then educate the buying group on the reasons it is worth it and how you can help mitigate those risks.

As I mentioned earlier in the book, research shows that objections lengthen the sales cycle by several months, so the earlier you educate your buyers on overcoming objections, the faster the purchase decision becomes. And, as a side benefit, it's a less painful emotional experience for your buyers. Because you bring those common pitfalls up early, before they become concerns, buyers perceive those as educational experiences rather than concerns that were addressed.

Many salespeople will make a list of common objections and how to handle them. I suggest you take it a step further and organize the list by role and stage of buying process. Think of objections as frequently asked questions (FAQs), and guide your buying group to the questions and answers they should be thinking about.

If a typical buying group consists of an end user, marketing leader, human resources leader, IT professional, C-level leader, and legal, you would need to personalize stories, demos, and so on for each of those roles. The end user may have questions about ease of use or how your solution integrates with their favorite email system. The IT professional wants to know how it meets GDPR requirements. These are just a couple of examples of the many questions that can come up.

Personalize the concerns and questions that come up by role so that you and your internal champion know how to address them. Equip your internal champion with these personalized FAQs to be prepared for concerns that frequently come up when they evangelize inside their organization. Not only will this prevent them from being caught off guard as often, but it will also build confidence in you as the trusted partner. (Not sure where to start? I've put together some ideas to get you started on this in the "Risks to Consider and Mitigation Strategies" template recommended in the Appendix.)

Use Digital Options to Engage in Appointment Gaps and Shorten the Sales Cycle

Let's do a thought experiment. Assume you have a 180-day sales cycle. How much of that time is made up of the gaps between appointments? Suppose the 180 days involves 12 live conversations that are, on average, two weeks apart. That means there are 168 days where your buying group is in between appointments! What are they doing during that time? Usually they are losing momentum, that's what.

If you use digital content options, these gaps provide a huge opportunity to maintain momentum, keep the buying group engaged and focused, and discover and engage other stakeholders.

But what kinds of digital content should you share during those gaps? The buyer enablement perspective gives us the answer: You should be recommending them content relevant to their stage in the buying process and to their buying persona that will help them with the current buying tasks they are working on.

Obviously this means that to know what content to engage them with "in the gap," you need to understand where they are at in the buying process and their persona.

As an example of these kinds of opportunities that these appointment gaps provide, ask yourself how you are engaging your prospects between the first appointment you set and when it is actually held. Are you just following up to see if they will hold the appointment? If so, it's a missed opportunity. What kind of content can you send and recommend to them to review and share with other stakeholders before you meet in the live conversation? If they do engage with that content and share it with others before that first appointment, how will it change the nature of that live conversation?

The answer is that you maintain momentum, have more meaningful live conversations (because buyers come ready to talk specifics), discover and engage other stakeholders sooner, and shorten the sales cycle.

Superior Engagement Through Buyer Enablement

The generally accepted way to discover stakeholders is to ask your champion who else needs to get involved, and rely on their judgment. The buyer enablement approach requires us to first map out the stakeholders based on our experience in the buying process, collaborate with the champion to identify the specific individuals who match the buying personas in the buying group map, and then proactively engage them with questions, listening, and content that educates them based on their unique perspective. You can do this manually or use buyer enablement technology to accelerate the process.

CHAPTER 8

DEEP-C: EQUIP YOUR CHAMPION

"By failing to prepare, you are preparing to fail."

—BENJAMIN FRANKLIN

Remember when you were a kid? What was the first thing you wanted to do when you learned something new? Run and tell someone—usually a parent or a friend. We aren't that different as adults. If you've gained the prospect's trust and educated them effectively, they will want to go sell for you internally. They are excited to do so. You and your solution are going to help them and their firm solve a critical problem or reach an important goal. So naturally they want to run out and tell everyone what they've found.

The problem, as I've discussed several times, is that they aren't ready. Imagine pulling someone off the street and asking them to sell your solution with just two to three hours of training. While your champion is probably more able than a random person off the street, this analogy illustrates the challenges they face. They haven't been through your company's training; they don't know how to ask the right questions or personalize their excited pitch to the unique needs of each stakeholder.

They usually run into all kinds of concerns and obstacles that they aren't prepared for and consequently come back to you with dampened enthusiasm.

Champions inside organizations don't like being hung out to dry.

According to Gartner, "Eighty percent of the B2B mobilizers whom CEB (now Gartner) surveyed said they wanted support from suppliers in communicating the value of the solutions they champion."[1]

To enable your champion to sell for you, it's your job to equip them with the information they need at the times they need it and coach them as they sell internally for you.

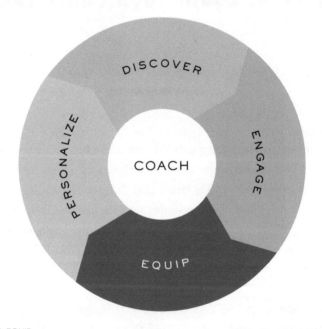

Figure 24: EQUIP.

The Challenge of Communication Overload

A common "sales enablement" approach is to create an online deal room that has everything the champion needs. At first glance, this

---

1   Gartner, *Tech Go-to-Market: Why Tech Sales Cycles Are Taking So Long and What Needs to Be Done Now*, Michele Buckley, June 4, 2018.

sounds great, but it leaves the prospect to dig through mountains of information that usually isn't organized in ways that make referencing information they need easy (such as by role in the buying group or organizational position). For example, when an end user enters the deal room, they are looking for content that is quite different from what a CFO would be looking for.

Building a deal room that presents the same content for many different stakeholders is the "sales enablement" approach: It puts the burden on the buyers to sift through material to find what is relevant to them.

A Gartner survey asked organizations, "What is the one thing tech providers could do to make buying easier?" "A Gartner survey found the most frequently cited (free form) response to the question of 'what is the one thing tech providers could do to make buying easier?' was improved information—by an overwhelming margin."[2]

While access to great information is what buyers want, throwing too much information or information that isn't suited for the stage of the buying cycle the buyers are in will just confuse them and cause them to throw up their hands in exasperation.

Verbose approaches are effectively telling buyers, "Here is everything you could ever possibly want to know, but it is up to you to figure out what matters." However, the reality is that most customers don't have the time or patience to figure out what matters. Your goal is to make the buying process easier for buyers, rather than adding to their workload.

Kristin Nagel, senior account manager at ZoomInfo, agrees. "In my experience, I have found that coaching my customers through the buying process and enabling them to make a good decision that they are comfortable with drastically reduces my sales cycle and improves close rates. I'm all about making buying easy for the customer instead of just dumping a bunch of information in their lap and letting them sort it out," she said.[3]

---

2   Gartner, Tech Go-to-Market: 4 Steps to a Differentiated Messaging Foundation, Mark Stanyer, Hank Barnes, Michael Maziarka, May 17, 2018.
3   Kristin Nagel, in discussion with the author, March 23, 2018.

What Kinds of Information and Tools Do Your Champions Need?

Going back to the analogy of taking an exploratory expedition up into the Amazon—before you left, you would want to make a list of supplies and equipment, sorted by what is needed at different stages of the journey. In sales, the equivalent concept is having a detailed list of information that each member of the buying group needs at each stage of the buying process.

Start by mapping your buying group personas, and then ask yourself, "What questions does this persona need answered before they can make a purchase?"

In the previous chapter, we discussed the questions the buying group needs answers to. Said another way, every stakeholder in the buying group needs to agree:

- That the problem needs fixing

- That the problem needs fixing now

- That the solution the champion is proposing is the right solution to address the problem

- That the specific vendor the champion is advocating is the right choice

- That the financial return on investment (ROI) is worth it

- That questions and concerns specific to their differing roles have been resolved

- That there is adequate social proof that other similar companies are achieving good results

- That there is a viable implementation plan following the purchase

What kinds of information will help stakeholders reach those conclusions?

It turns out that many different types of information can help (Figure 25).

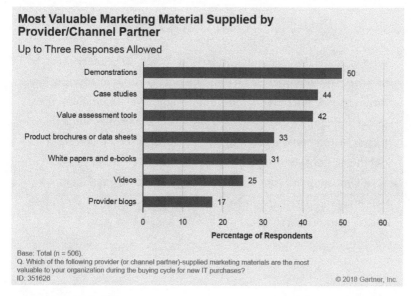

Figure 25: "Most Valuable Marketing Material Supplied by Provider/Channel Partner" according to Gartner.[4]

In terms of buyer enablement, there are seven categories of information that I consider essential for the buyers to have a successful journey:

1. Evaluation guides

2. Personalized demos by role

3. Personalized FAQs by role

4. ROI calculations

5. Social proof by relevant role, segment, and industry

6. Implementation guides and templates

7. Materials for secondary (but critical) stakeholders

Let's take a look at each of these tools in more detail.

---

4   Gartner, Tech Go-to-Market: Content That Builds Trust and Delivers Value Can Influence Shortlist and Vendor Selection, Christy Ferguson, Todd Berkowitz, August 2, 2019.

WHO CREATES ALL OF THIS CONTENT?

Who creates the content depends on what kind of content is needed. This all depends on the different personas in your buying group map. If the persona only needs high-level information, then marketing may be creating the content. If the persona needs deep technical information, you may need to involve someone from IT to get the content your buyer persona needs.

As you map out your content strategy based on buyer personas, you may want to jot down who in your organization (or what role) will be responsible for creating the content.

Evaluation Guides

The first thing an adventurer about to take a trip along the Amazon would want to know is different routes they can take, what to expect, what dangers they might encounter, and how they might prepare. Similarly, as a buying coach, you need to provide a guide for how to compare and evaluate products in your industry. You could, for example, describe the major problems your buyers are often trying to solve, what kinds of technologies or solutions are available to solve them, how different technologies apply to different situations, when and how different members of the buying group get involved, the role of free trials or freemium options, the key questions they should be asking as they evaluate, and maybe even a scoring mechanism for evaluating different solution providers.

As an example, HubSpot provides prospects with a series of assets, including a slide deck titled "The Ultimate Kit for Convincing Your CFO." That "ultimate kit" explains what is top of mind for the CFO, the main value proposition from the CFO's perspective, what concerns or objections they might have, and so on. It's a guide for the CFO in particular because HubSpot knows that the CFO almost always has to get involved to get the purchase over the finish line.

Personalized Demos by Role

Getting your buyers to believe the problem needs fixing, that it needs fixing right now, and that your solution can help is largely an educational challenge. Your champion needs to educate the stakeholders on the financial and nonquantitative costs of *not* addressing the problem. They need and want support from you in selling the value inside their organization.

Equipping your champion with a product demonstration is one of the best ways to help stakeholders rally around a specific vendor's solution. During the demo, the best salespeople and solution consultants continue to learn more about each stakeholder, teasing out some of the alignment or misalignment in interests, commitment to solving the problem, and more. In this way, the demo becomes about much more than just educating your buyer—it is a data-rich interactive experience that provides you and the champion with key takeaways.

A popular way to fill this need is to give the champion access to PDF documents organized by role. In this instance, the reps need to coach the champion on which documents to share with which stakeholders (and when) and hope that the documents engage the stakeholders effectively.

A better approach is to consider equipping your champion with an automated product demonstration. The champion is provided a link to an interactive video demo that generates a unique video based on role and specific interests of the stakeholder who is using the link. This is a more effective approach because the champion only needs to forward the same link, and the demo automation platform automatically adjusts the content to the stakeholder's role and interests.

An automated demo is *not* a canned demo recording, such as a YouTube or WebEx recording. To effectively engage with the stakeholders being contacted by your champion, your demo automation platforms needs to:

- Ask questions to discover the role, as well as the unique interests, of each stakeholder
- Customize the resulting demo based on those results
- Display a map of engagement across the buying group that helps shine a light on alignment or misalignment

THE AUTOMATED DEMO BECOMES THE PROXY SALES REP

Because the champion is not a professional salesperson, the automated demos must play that role for them. As I talked about in the previous chapter, you must:

- Raise awareness about the pain they are experiencing
- Create urgency (why it's important to solve the problem now, including the cost of delays and inaction)
- Make it clear what your solution accomplishes and why your solution is better than the competition's

Personalized FAQs by Role

Does the CFO have different questions or concerns than the end user? Does the middle manager have different concerns than the IT department? Of course! And your champion needs to be adept at anticipating and answering the many different kinds of questions they will field from each persona in the buying group.

Many vendors provide an FAQ page on their website, but it is usually inadequate and largely superficial. Most buyers find that FAQs don't answer the most important questions about buying. Because of your (and your team's) experience guiding dozens of buyers through the purchasing process, you know which questions most often surface from each persona. In light of this, you should equip your champion with one of the following:

- A document or set of documents that detail the most often heard questions and answers for each role in the buying group (a good start, but an old-school approach).

- Dynamic personalized FAQs using buyer enablement technology that automatically adjusts the questions and answers based on role. This way, when the champion fields a question, they can say, "Let me check on that and get back to you." Then they can forward a link to an FAQ that addresses the stakeholder's specific question. As the stakeholder engages with that specific question and answer, the technology also prompts them to explore other commonly asked questions by buyers in similar roles. This technology also tracks who is engaging with what questions the most, providing valuable data analytics back to the sales and marketing teams.

- A series of videos showing the answers to FAQs. This can be especially helpful for difficult concepts or if the questions pertain to the product.

You should also encourage the champion to preempt the questions by leading with: "Here are some of the frequently asked questions and concerns that come up for others in your role. Take a look at these, and then let's get on a call with the vendor to discuss any further details you might have questions about." By exerting leadership in this way, you are demonstrating that you are the valued partner—to the champion and to the stakeholder.

ROI Calculations

At some point, most or all of the stakeholders in the buying group need to agree that the financial investment in the solution or product is worth making. In fact, 89% of buyers in a recent survey stated that winning vendors "provided content that made it easier to show ROI and/or build a business case for the purchase."[5] That's nine out of ten buyers who found it important that the vendor help them make the business case.

Most salespeople engage in some kind of ROI calculations during the B2B sales process. Make sure to equip your champion with an ROI calculation and calculator that can be shared with other stakeholders. Here are some tips for effective ROI calculations and calculators with which to equip your champion:

- Simpler calculators will get more engagement than complex calculators.

- Share it in a way that is easy to consume. This can take the form of a PDF report or an interactive calculator online.

- If possible, share the ROI calculation in a way that each stakeholder can adjust the inputs. Stakeholders are often skeptical of the inputs provided by the sales team or the champion and want to evaluate based on their own assumptions.

I would also recommend using a technology that can track who is engaging with the ROI calculator. If a stakeholder isn't engaging, it's possible they don't care about the financial ROI, but more likely, it is an indication that they are not vested in the evaluation yet and need more nurturing. If the technology can track the inputs of each stakeholder, so much the better. This will provide immensely useful data to see the different perspectives the stakeholders bring to the ROI evaluation. That's information you can share with your champion to help them deal more effectively with each stakeholder.

---

5   "2017 B2B Buyer Survey Report," Demand Gen,
    https://www.demandgenreport.com/resources/research/2017-b2b-buyers-survey-report.

FROM MICHAEL FARBER, FOUNDER OF THE ROI SHOP

Sitting down with your prospect and building the financial business case is one of the most important meetings you can have during the sales cycle. Let's face it—companies are going to make a purchasing decision for two main reasons:

- To make money
- To save money

The unfortunate truth is that if your sales reps are leaving it up to their champions to quantify your benefits, you will continue to lose 40%–60% of all your opportunities to "no decision."

Since founding The ROI Shop, I've partnered with over 70 companies, and more than 85% of them had a hard time *clearly* quantifying their benefits to me. Think about that for a second. These companies eat, sleep, and breathe their solution 24/7, and they still struggle to clearly communicate their true financial impact. If the experts can't clearly lay out the financial benefits, how can you expect your champion to be successful when they have been exposed to your offering for only an hour or two?

When I ask a prospect, "How do you help your customers make or save money?" sadly, the coined response is often "We save the salesperson time and they can use that time to sell more," and that is the extent of it.

Obviously, that is not quantifying your benefits, and that's certainly not arming your champion to sell the project internally.

Using the above scenario, it is much more impactful to guide your prospect through a series of questions that can help calculate an actual number of hours a salesperson would save. Once there is agreement on the time savings, you can apply a financial value to those hours. Now you have armed your champion with a compelling story to share when asking for a budget.

Social Proof by Relevant Role, Segment, and Industry

Few of us want to be the guinea pigs for some new solution. We much prefer at least some evidence that the solution we're considering has been proven successful with others. Evidence that others similar to us have experienced similar problems and succeeded at solving them is what we call social proof. "Proof" because it's evidence that the solution works. "Social" because it is working for other people we consider to be in similar categories.

TYPES OF SOCIAL PROOF

You may recall that social proof includes any media that captures stories of real people solving problems similar to what the prospect is facing. This can include white papers, case studies, quotes, video testimonials, references, and online review sites.

How Do I Equip My Champion with Powerful Social Proof?

To equip your champion with powerful social proof, first answer these questions:

- What is the title, title level, and role of the stakeholder who needs the proof?
- What is the problem the champion is trying to solve (or opportunity they are trying to take advantage of)? In other words, what is their "use case"?
- What is the unique perspective the role of the stakeholder typically brings to the buying analysis?

- What is the size of the company? Is it small business, midmarket, enterprise, or very large enterprise?
- What is the industry?

Once you have the answers to these questions, be sure to tag your social proof case studies so the prospect can easily locate the examples that most closely match their circumstances. The closer the content of your social proof matches each of the answers to these questions, the more powerful the social proof will be.

To illustrate, let's look at an example from the consumer world, and then we'll bring it back to B2B. Suppose a mom and dad are trying to buy a car for their teen daughter. Each of the parents is tired of driving their daughter around, and they want their teen to be able to go places on her own. However, each parent has different concerns about making the purchase. In other words, there are risks, and risks are the inherent reason buyers need social proof.

Let's suppose that the questions and concerns break down like this:

- Safety: Mom is concerned that her kid is going to joyride into a wall.
- Insurance: Dad is concerned that insurance costs are going to go way up.
- Teaching Responsibility: Both Mom and Dad are hoping that owning a car will teach the teen some responsibility because the teen has to care for the car and deal with making more responsible decisions.
- Pros and Cons to Autonomy: Dad wants to understand the pros and cons of giving the teen additional autonomy. Will the child abuse it? Will it create new opportunities for employment, sports, or school activities for the child?
- Taking Your Life Back: Both Mom and Dad are excited about the prospect of the extra time they will have each week because they no longer have to play the role of taxi driver.

Now suppose you, as a car dealer, know some other things about this family: The parents are middle-income, educated, in their mid-forties, and living in a large city. Pretty quickly, it's clear that your champion in this situation is Dad. He has chosen one of the models you sell as a perfect match for his concerns. He's trying to convince Mom, but Mom is still concerned about safety and not quite yet on board. You decide to provide Dad with video testimonials. Here are two scenarios:

Scenario 1

You provide video testimonials of fathers from farming communities talking about how they taught their sons to drive and how that has helped them on the farm and safety incidents were practically nonexistent.

While somewhat helpful because it addresses the safety question, you can see that the title (father vs. mother), use case (learning to drive to be helpful rather than free up time), gender (son vs. daughter), and segment (rural vs. urban) are wrong. So while it might have some impact, Mom is most likely to view that proof point with some skepticism or consider it largely irrelevant.

Scenario 2

You equip Dad with a video testimonial of three mothers: one from Los Angeles, California; one from Chicago, Illinois; and one from London, UK. Each of them spoke about helping their daughters gain confidence and have new experiences. Each spoke of their concerns about safety and how the car they chose, equipped with new teen-specific features, helped them know where their teen was, when they exceeded the speed limit, and how many people were in the car. The more similar the title, role, segment, and use case, the more power the social proof carries. This scenario did the trick.

This is true in B2B as well. If your target stakeholder is an SVP of HR inside a midmarket company looking for HR software because they want to handle payroll and compensation more effectively, and you send them a case study of a small business HR manager who bought your HR management software to improve the hiring process, it's not going to have the impact you expect.

Consider that you need to provide the right kind of social proof for each stakeholder in the buying group. This requires a significant effort on your part to create and deliver the right types and numbers of social proof to your champion.

TECHNOLOGY TIP

As a rule of thumb, attempt to build a database of at least three pieces of social proof that match each persona title, industry, company size, and use case combination. The reason you need three is because you may use one for lead gen and then the other two to equip the champion as they sell internally to that stakeholder persona.

Use the Social Proof Resource Map Toolkit that can be found on our website, buyerenablement.io, to uncover gaps. Then go to work finding social proof that matches up.

When Should the Champion Use Social Proof Resources?

As the buying-process coach, you want to preemptively address any concerns that are likely to arise. While I don't suggest that you encourage the champion to share all social proof up front, at least some social proof early in the process is good for them to share with the other stakeholders to help put their minds at ease. Then as you and your champion progress each stakeholder forward, carefully suggest social proof points the champion can share that bolster the use case you're striving to implement for that organization.

In short, share at the beginning and then in the middle of the process. Then, if there is any late-stage resistance, your third piece of social proof can help increase stakeholder confidence near the end of the deal.

TECHNOLOGY TIP

Consider putting your testimonial videos inside an automated demo that allows the stakeholder to customize based on their role and interests. That way your champion can share one link with each stakeholder, and they'll automatically get the social proof points they need while you get rich data analytics as that engagement is tracked across multiple buying processes.

Implementation Guides and Templates

Your champion needs your help even more desperately after the purchase. Their reputation is now on the line to deliver the value they touted. Consider providing them step-by-step guides on how to implement and start seeing value as quickly as possible. Look through your currently successful customers, and ask yourselves and them what worked for them. Turn this into a guide or template that your new customers can follow.

CROSS REFERENCE

See Chapter 11, "Continue Champion Enablement After the Purchase," for more ideas on this stage of buyer enablement.

See buyerenablement.io for an example of an implementation guide we use at Consensus.

Materials for Secondary (but Critical) Stakeholders

As I've mentioned, don't forget to consider the needs of secondary stakeholders, such as representatives from finance, IT, and legal. You will need to provide your champion with materials that preemptively address the most common needs of these roles as well. This might include things such as:

- An information security packet that includes things like these:
  - Your end user agreement and privacy policy
  - Your detailed security policy
  - Your most recent penetration test results
  - Your general data protection regulation (GDPR) compliance documentation
  - Your service organization control 2 (SOC 2) or other similar compliance documentation
- A pro forma invoice for the finance department to review
- A sample contract to get in for early review by the legal team (or if legal requires you to sign on their paper, get a contract sample from them to have the appropriate parties on your side begin reviewing it)

The earlier your champion can engage these stakeholders, the faster the purchase will get done. As an example, just a few days ago I provided materials designed to answer the most common questions we get about information security to the champion on a certain deal. I asked him if he could provide them to the IT department (I was trying to preempt the 300-plus-line questionnaire I knew was coming), and I got this response back:

Thanks to your quick response and what you provided previously, [the IT department] bypassed the questionnaire. I received confirmation this morning that we've moved the process to the next stage!

This saved at least two to three weeks of back-and-forth with the IT department.

Beyond accelerating the specific deal, having these materials at the ready that are targeted to the secondary stakeholders shows that you are a competent organization, and will increase confidence that you will be a solid vendor.

Be Engaging and Persuasive

I'm going to challenge you to ask yourself, "Do I equip my champions with the materials they need to be successful internally, or do I often see them not succeeding when they make the attempt to educate their peers and colleagues?"

The key point of this chapter is that your organization must understand the questions the buying group needs answers to and have diverse mechanisms for engaging your champion around those questions so they can subsequently reach other stakeholders. Each mechanism—automated demo, online resources, and so on—must fill a niche by addressing the perspectives, interests, and needs of specific stakeholders. When you have this arsenal ready, you can best equip your champion to do battle for you.

CHAPTER 9

DEEP-C: PERSONALIZE VALUE

"Remember that a person's name is to that person the sweetest
and most important sound in any language."
—DALE CARNEGIE

We love to hear our names, especially when spoken sincerely. When used insincerely, we almost feel insulted. In college, I sang in audition choirs at Brigham Young University in Utah. I sang under a director named Mack Wilberg, who now conducts one of the world's most famous choirs, The Tabernacle Choir at Temple Square. Mack is an incredible talent. Not only is he an inspiring conductor, gifted arranger, and overall musical genius, but he also has the amazing ability to remember everyone's name.

At first glance, you may think, *Well, that's great, but I know lots of people who are good at remembering names. What is so special about that?* What I mean is that Mack remembered everyone's name, all of the time, and for years on end. He had over 350 students singing in the two choirs that he conducted. After my freshman year, I left to serve my church, the Church of Jesus Christ of Latter-day Saints, as a missionary in Argentina. When I came back, I wanted to audition for Mack's men's chorus, one of the most popular performing groups on campus. As I walked up the stairs of the fine arts building to his office to see if I could find any posted flyers about auditions, I was nervous. I had been gone for two years. I had been immersed in a completely different culture and language and had only arrived back home a week earlier. I was still getting my feet under me.

As I turned the corner leading to his office, I literally bumped into Mack. "Oh! I'm sorry," I said. Without hesitation he said, "Oh, hello, Garin. It is great to see you. I haven't seen you in a while. How was Argentina?"

I was astonished that he remembered my name after two years away. I instantly felt more at ease and more confident around him. It turns out he was able to do that with everyone whom he worked with. Using names is a common type of personalization.

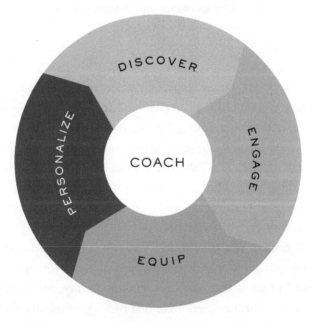

Figure 26: PERSONALIZE.

Adult-Learning Theory and the Need for Relevance

A large part of the buying process is educating stakeholders. You need to teach your champion, and your champion needs to teach the other stakeholders. Adult-learning theory is the body of research that investigates the most effective ways that adults learn and, consequently, how we should teach adults when we're in a teaching role.

In a great article on adult-learning theory published by the Association for Talent Development, Karla Gutierrez summarizes several research-based approaches to teaching adults.[1] In both the andragogy approach ("pedagogy" is teaching children and "andragogy" is teaching adults), which points out the differences in how adults learn versus how children learn, and the transformative-learning approach, which challenges adults to challenge their beliefs and use their critical-thinking skills, her research suggests we have to establish relevance and motivation by addressing "what's in it for me" for the adult learner.

In other words, adult learners don't care about a subject until they can connect the dots to how it creates value for them personally. Your solution might solve a problem for them, open up an opportunity, or make their life easier in some way, but their problems and opportunities often differ from others in the buying group. In short, adults crave relevance. So we salespeople need to deliver a personalized buying experience not just for the champion but also for every stakeholder in the group.

There is now an established body of evidence that personalization has a massive impact on getting B2B buying groups to make it through the buying journey successfully. Here is a sampling of recent findings:

---

1 Karla Gutierrez, "3 Adult Learning Theories Every E-Learning Designer Must Know," Association for Talent Development, January 26, 2018, https://www.td.org/insights/3-adult-learning-theories-every-e-learning-designer-must-know.

- Personalization yields 40% higher purchase intent.[2] (A B2C statistic shows that 35% of Amazon's revenue is due to personalized recommendations.)[3]

- Personalization brings 30% higher close rates.[4]

- 82% of buyers feel more positive about a company with personalized content.[5]

- 74% of buyers get frustrated when content doesn't have to do with their interests.[6]

"Don't Waste My Time"

Core to adults' needs for personalization is not only relevance but also respect for the value of their time. Just think how quickly we bounce from Google search results if we don't see what is relevant. Quite often, we won't spend even a few seconds searching the second page for something relevant because we don't want to spend the time.

How often have you been in the role of prospect in a sales presentation or demo and thought to yourself, *This is a waste of my time?* You should remember this and then realize that the goal with every

2   Karl Schmidt, Brent Adamson, and Anna Bird, "Making the Consensus Sale," *Harvard Business Review*, March 2015, https://hbr.org/2015/03/making-the-consensus-sale.

3   "The Amazon Recommendations Secret to Selling More Online," Rejoiner, blog, http://rejoiner.com/resources/amazon-recommendations-secret-selling-online/.

4   Seismic, "Succeed in 2019 by Personalizing and Automating Your Sales Content," MarketingProfs, September 17, 2018, https://www.marketingprofs.com /articles/2018/39778/succeed-in-2019-by-personalizing-and-automating-your-sales-content.

5   Adam Deflorian, "Loyal to Content: Thinking Beyond Punch Cards for Loyalty Programs," *Forbes*, September 27, 2018, https://www.forbes.com/sites /forbesagencycouncil/2018/09/27/loyal-to-content-thinking-beyond-punch-cards -for-loyalty-programs/#42c759b24666.

6   "Online Consumers Fed Up with Irrelevant Content on Favorite Websites, According to Janrain Study," MarketWatch press release, July 31, 2013, https://www.marketwatch.com /press-release/online-consumers-fed-up-with-irrelevant-content-on-favorite-websites- according-to-janrain-study-2013-07-31.

interaction is to give buyers an Emotional ROI. If they invest their time, what do they get in return? Any amount of time they have to spend with you on content that is not relevant to them reduces their Emotional ROI.

Delivering personalized content shows that you are respectful of their time. Ask questions, and then personalize your approach. Too often, we have topics or features that we want to cover because *we* think they are so great. I've seen otherwise excellent sales reps lose their buyer's motivation by asking good questions resulting in great interactive discovery, then veering off subject to talk about their favorite topics, which are unrelated to anything the customer mentioned.

Gimmicky vs. Meaningful Personalization

Our objective is to discover, engage, and personalize our stakeholder education and collaboration. What kind of personalization will get stakeholders to engage meaningfully over time?

Superficial "Gimmicky" Personalization

Research by Experian marketing services shows that when you see your name in a subject line, you are 29% more likely to open the email.[7] Even scamming spammers know this, which is why you see subject lines like "Jack, your long-lost relative has left you $4 billion."

While this type of "personalization" does yield some results, this is what I call superficial or gimmicky personalization. It's not personalizing the value; it's only personalizing to catch your attention. It does work, and yes, in your outreach you should remember that someone's name is important to them. But remember that buyers want to know

---

7   Mary Fernandez, "164 Best Email Subject Lines to Boost Your Email Open Rates (2019)," Optinmonster, July18, 2019, https://optinmonster.com/101-email-subject-lines-your-subscribers-cant-resist/.

what's in it for them, so you need to personalize based on the interests unique to each decision maker's persona profile.

Gimmicky personalization is superficial. Personalizing the value content is meaningful.

Personalizing the Value Message to Each Stakeholder

Moving beyond superficial personalization means personalizing the message in a way that resonates with each stakeholder's unique interests. Since 74% of buyers get frustrated when content is not personalized to their interests, it's a mission-critical skill. What percentage of salespeople in your organization can do this effectively?

Tamara Schenk of CSO Insights has summarized differences between world-class salespeople and the rest of the field.[8] She points out that:

- different decision makers perceive value and relevance differently, and

- successful value messages are tailored to each decision maker's value profile to gain access and create a future vision of success.

Schenk's article evaluated the percentage of salespeople who mastered this ability. The answer? An astonishingly low 7.7%. That means that 92.3% of salespeople do not master tailoring value messages to each decision maker (isn't that another way of saying "practically everyone"?). In short, less than one in ten salespeople master one of the most important skills in B2B sales.

Even more troubling is that if only 7.7% of experienced B2B sales professionals master this skill, what percentage of champions are able to customize the message while they engage the different stakeholders inside their own organization? Probably close to 0%!

---

8   Tamara Shenk, "How to Gain Access to Key Decision Makers: What World-Class Performers Do Differently," CSO Insights, blog, July 14, 2016, https://www.csoinsights.com /blog/how-to-gain-access-to-key-decision-makers-what-world-class-performers-do-differently.

So the question you need to answer is "How do I equip and coach the champion in a way that they can deliver personalized messages throughout the buying process?"

There are two ways to get the unskilled 92% of your sales team and the champions they work with more capable in this mission-critical area: in-depth training or giving them an assist through the use of content and technology designed to meet the personalization needs of different stakeholders. A mix of both is probably important for your sales team.

For your champion, in-depth training is not an option, so you need to equip them with a mix of content and technology. For both your sales reps and your champions, technology can decrease the need to rely on training and skill. It helps fill the gap.

The Potential for Overdoing Personalization

In the book *The Challenger Customer*, Brent Adamson and his coauthors suggest that overemphasis on personalizing content can sometimes backfire.[9] Their research suggests that tailoring too much to the unique needs of each stakeholder can cause them to overly focus on the differences between their needs and the other needs in the buying group—which can lead to misalignment rather than agreement. Each personalization effort needs to be linked back to the main problem everyone is trying to solve. Remember, all the stakeholders want to solve the problem, but they have different angles on what the problem and the solution means based on their roles.

While overdoing personalization may be something to be on the lookout for, in my opinion this warning is a bit of a paper tiger given that more than 90% of your sales teams are not skilled at personalizing content effectively in the first place. What is the bigger problem: that most of your team and your champion isn't personalizing the

---

9   Brent Adamson, Matthew Dixon, Pat Spenner, and Nick Toman, *The Challenger Customer: Selling to the Hidden Influencer Who Can Multiply Your Results* (New York City: Portfolio, 2015).

content or that they are over-personalizing? It's an interesting find-ing, but my recommendation is to first ensure that your team is able to personalize the content effectively, but verify that it is driving the effectiveness that you are looking for.

Building Personalized Buyer Enablement Content

To build personalized content that will meet the needs of each stake-holder, first identify the gaps, then build, distribute, and train on the content. To drive the use of personalized buyer enablement content, you must once again start from having a map of the buying group personas and then perform the following six steps, as depicted in Figure 27.

Figure 27: Creating Personalized Content: Most organizations won't go to the effort of creating per-sonalized content by role. Make the effort and you'll instantly have the competitive advantage.

1. Identify your content library gaps in the areas of educational content, objection resolution, social proof, and task facilitation. (For example, what tasks do your buyers need to complete, and what content can help them complete them?)

2. Identify the 7.7% of people on your staff who are adept at personalizing content and messages.

3. With input from those you identify in step two, make a content development plan to complete the buyer enablement content strategy.

4. Begin building the content.

5. Make the content accessible for the sales team, and train them on how to use it and how to equip and coach their champions to use it.

6. Begin to measure how the content is used, and track buyer enablement metrics to measure the number of stakeholders discovered, engagement, and impact on sales cycles and close rates.

Repeat the process as you discover more gaps. In this way you grow your buyer enablement library.

TIP

Some personas in the buying group are much more influential and important to getting a decision made than other personas. Identify those personas first, and enable your champion with content specifically for them.

Personalize to the Persona or the Person?

Personalizing content has often been the realm of marketing rather than sales. Marketing has long advocated for personalizing content to the persona, meaning targeting a specific *type* of buyer based on a detailed description of characteristics shared by the roles in the target audience. The ultimate goal in marketing is to generate qualified leads for the sales team.

In sales, we have to take personalizing a step further and target not just the initial lead but also the personas of each role in the buying group (see Figure 28).

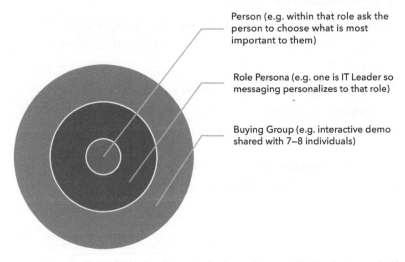

Person (e.g. within that role ask the person to choose what is most important to them)

Role Persona (e.g. one is IT Leader so messaging personalizes to that role)

Buying Group (e.g. interactive demo shared with 7–8 individuals)

Figure 28: Increasing Levels of Personalization: Technology makes it possible to make content deeply relevant to each individual at scale.

With the rise of technology comes this question: Can we move beyond customizing content to the persona and customize the content to each person? If customizing content to the persona is targeted messaging, personalizing to the person is *ultra-targeted messaging.*

Because personas share similar interests, targeting the persona with tailored messaging can have dramatic effect. When Consensus customers use advanced branching features in their interactive demos to discover the persona and target the message to them, their engagement rates almost always double overnight.[10] Without a doubt, targeting messaging to the persona is powerful. But can we take it a step further?

Personalizing the Message to the Person (or Individual)

Even though personas are a group of individuals that share common characteristics, each individual in that group will still have their own unique interests, so we should endeavor to target to the individual as well.

The simplest way of doing this is to ask them questions about what interests them uniquely. If there is a set of questions and topics that interest that persona group, knowing that individual's unique interests allows you to not only target their general domain of content but also personalize down to the very specific sections of content driving that person's purchasing interests.

TIP

Once you or your champion has engaged the stakeholder with a message that is unique to the persona group they belong to, break that general area of content into subsections and ask the stakeholder to rate whether each section is very important, somewhat important, or not important. Then you have clear knowledge of exactly what kinds of content are at the top of their minds. Lead with the very important information, going into great detail; follow this with touching on the content that is somewhat important to them; and finally, skip the content that is not important to them.

---

10 Engagement data as tracked by Consensus intelligent demo automation software.

Without the use of technology, this would be largely impossible to do at scale, but new software that supports buyer enablement has the capacity to assist by handling this personalization automatically. In addition, as each role and each champion engages over hundreds of opportunities, technology can show patterns and trends to give you deeper insights into your target audience's preferences and behavior.

What's at the Core of Personalization?

At the core of our desire for personalization is our need to know three things:

1. People care.

2. What they have to share with us is relevant.

3. People are interested in helping us make the best use of our time.

When it comes to dealing with potential buyers, it is your behavior that will demonstrate whether you genuinely care about them. The fact that you want them to make the best use of their time will be an outcome of how relevant the information that you provide is to them. And relevance comes through personalization. That's why personalization is a critical component of buyer enablement.

CHAPTER 10

DEEP-C: COACH YOUR CHAMPION

"Leadership is a matter of having people look at you and gain confidence . . . if you're in control, they're in control."

—TOM LANDRY

Core to buyer enablement is a fundamental shift in how you think about yourself. Are you a seller or a buying coach? As we've discussed, even though the buyers are the people who can close the deal, they don't know how to do it. You have to lead them.

That means your most valuable contributions to the buying process will be in the form of coaching, not selling. It's a role you will need to play throughout the buying process (see Figure 29).

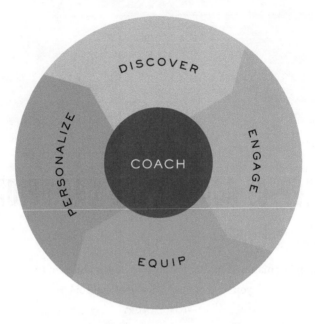

Figure 29: COACH.

What Does the Champion Need Coaching On?

Your champion needs to know, at a minimum:

- The process of getting the purchase completed
- The tasks they need to complete to get the purchase completed
- The obstacles they will encounter and how to prepare for and overcome them
- What roles need to get involved and the questions and concerns they will bring to the table

The Buyer Enablement Coaching Process: Recommend, Commit, Facilitate

Think of the buying process like a full-length sports match. You're the coach. You need to recruit your star players to win the game. If it were a basketball game, you might first recruit your point guard (your champion). Unlike a sporting match, you'll recruit the rest of your team (stakeholders) as time moves forward. Each team member will help you get the deal done in one way or another, though some stakeholders will appear to prevent it as they bring up what seems like pesky obstacles and even try to block the deal. The reality is that even those players help by bringing up valuable issues that need to be worked through.

During a sporting match, coaches are constantly giving advice, constantly engaging, asking for the players to commit to their guidance, and providing the resources and guidance necessary to win. Your role is similar. In the buying process, just like a sports coach, you can't win the game for your players. All you can do is help from the sidelines. You are a valued member of the team, but all you can do is *help* the players win the game.

To exert leadership as the buying coach in the purchasing process, follow these steps (see Figure 30):

1. Strongly recommend.

2. Ask the prospect (and other stakeholders where applicable) to commit.

3. Facilitate and be a resource.

Figure 30: Coaching Strategy: Most sellers are passive. As the buying coach, you need to exert leadership by committing your champion and other stakeholders to taking certain steps that you know will help them.

Strongly Recommend

The first step in the coaching process is to strongly recommend steps or actions—instead of waiting for your champion to tell you what they think. Relative to the DEEP components, this means:

- Discover: Recommend what roles need to be involved and recruit the buying group stakeholders.
- Engage: Recommend how to engage each stakeholder.
- Equip: Recommend what content should be given to what stakeholders and when and how they relate to tasks that need to be completed.

- Personalize: Recommend how to use the content to personalize to each stakeholder.

Key Phrases to Use When Recommending

At first, it might seem a little awkward to exert leadership and strongly recommend if you aren't used to it. So here are some phrases you can use to get started:

- "In my experience working with other companies trying to solve this challenge, I have found_____. I strongly recommend_____."
- "As we've worked with other firms going through this purchasing process, we have seen_____. For that reason here's what I'd like to propose_____."
- "If you don't mind, would it be all right with you if I offer some advice about what I see as the most effective process?"
- "In our experience, if we don't do X and Y, we are likely to run into challenges such as _____. I would like to prepare for these pitfalls by doing X and Y. Would that be okay with you?"
- "I really appreciate you sharing your thoughts about where we go from here. Do you mind if I share with you what I've seen as the next best steps at this stage in the buying process?"

By couching the recommendations in strong but deferential phrases, you're more likely to engage the champion and get them to follow your recommended steps. It makes them feel as if they are in control.

Invite the Champion to Commit

Winning a sports game requires a lot of strategizing, planning, and courageous and diligent execution. To win, a coach has to challenge his or her team. The same goes for you and your champion to make it successfully through a complex purchase.

We can imagine in a sports game that a coach might say something like, "Here's what we need to do:____. Now go out there and get it done." One time, my wife's high school basketball coach told her, "I want you to stick to that player like underwear! Got it?" My wife shouted, "You got it, Coach!" The visual of "as close as underwear" helped her play better defense, and her commitment to her coach kept her motivated through the rest of the game.

The coach not only needs to know what to do but also needs to commit the player to following that counsel. You need to do the same with your champion. Asking for commitments comes with the added benefit of providing you with clear data points about the true qualification and nature of the deal. Kevin Davis, author of *The Sales Manager's Guide to Greatness*, says:

> In many cases, the decision to buy represents a major commitment from the customer. Rather than expect that commitment to come all at once, surely it makes sense to have your salespeople ask for much less significant commitments along the way—such as agreeing to meetings, sharing information, and so on. If the customer doesn't agree to or follow through on the minor things, it's unlikely they will come through at the end with a major commitment.[1]

During the buying process, commitments your champion needs to make might include:

- Recruiting and introducing you to stakeholders
- Sharing key pieces of content materials with other stakeholders

---

1   Kevin F. Davis, *The Sales Manager's Guide to Greatness: 10 Essential Strategies for Leading Your Team to the Top* (Austin: Greenleaf Book Group, 2017): 106.

- Getting additional information specific to the target organization that you don't have
- Giving a presentation inside the target company
- Inviting stakeholders to key conversations where you can engage the stakeholders directly
- Following up to make sure the stakeholders are engaging
- Teasing out the question, concerns, and objections stakeholders may have
- Helping the stakeholders overcome their objections and concerns
- Asking for commitments from other stakeholders to get to a confident purchasing decision as quickly as possible

Key Phrases to Get Your Champion to Commit

Your role in the buying process is to get the champion to perform the actions that you know need to get done. To get a commitment from them, ask for it in a way that forces your champion to answer with a yes or no. Consider using the following phrases to get them to commit:

- "Will you . . ."
- "Would you be willing to . . ."
- "This is something best done by you as the internal advocate. Could you . . ."
- "In order to stay on our timeline, we'll need this by X date. Can you commit to this?"

My favorite is "Would you be willing to . . ." This phrase is deferential while exerting strong leadership and forces a direct yes or no answer.

One thing I love about asking for commitments is it is a moment of truth. The person either says yes and you move forward, or they say no and you begin to discover things about the deal that you didn't know before—things that are critical to getting the deal done.

If the answer is yes, great. Make sure to follow up and see if your champion is getting done whatever it is they committed to get done or if they need any additional help. Sometimes they run into roadblocks while they are making the effort. The more you follow up, the sooner you can enable the champion to overcome the roadblock.

If you get a no to your commitment request, don't be discouraged. Look at it as an opportunity because it's one of the best things that can happen to you in the buying process.

ACTION COMMITMENTS = EXIT CRITERIA

Kevin Davis calls action commitments "exit criteria," meaning the actions represent steps the customer must take to move forward in the buying process.[2] If the customer commits to and completes these actions, they have "exited" one step of buying and are moving on to the next step.

I always urge my sales staff to ask for a commitment to a specific timeline to make a decision. And once they've made the decision to move forward with a purchase, then ask for a commitment to close by a certain date. Remember, don't ask the customer to set the date. Instead, exert leadership and recommend a date that conforms with previous purchasing cycles you've seen in other buying groups. Then see how the customer responds. It goes something like this:

You: I think it's in both of our best interests to help you get to an effective decision as quickly as possible. Would you agree?

[You get a response, hopefully "yes."]

---

2   Davis, *The Sales Manager's Guide to Greatness*, p. 99.

You: We've found it extremely helpful to set a target date for making a final decision. Agreeing on this date will help you and me take the needed actions to move the decision-making process along. When other companies like yours have purchased our software, it usually takes three to four months to involve the appropriate stakeholders and get to a final decision. We can always adjust the target date as needs arise. Would you be willing to agree to an initial target date to make a decision one way or the other three months from now?

This phrasing leads to one of two outcomes I've discussed: They either commit to a specific timeline, or they tell you why they aren't ready for that. Both are great outcomes. If they do commit, you're on your way. If they don't commit, all of a sudden you know that you don't have a qualified opportunity and they aren't as serious as another opportunity that is ready to commit to making a decision by a specific date.

Whatever commitments you ask from your champion, if you get a no, you'll often get it indirectly. The champion will say something like, "Well, we're not quite ready for that" or "I don't really feel comfortable doing that." This will come up from time to time, but instead of feeling rejected, count it as an obstacle that needs overcoming. Sometimes it just means the champion needs more coaching to understand how to do what you're asking. Sometimes it means that you don't have the right champion. Sometimes they need more discussion, analysis, or education.

When you get a no, ask additional follow-up questions, such as:

- "Could you tell me more about that?"
- "What would it take to be able to get that done?"
- "Why do you think that won't be the most effective course of action right now?"
- "Would you mind telling me why you're not comfortable with these recommendations?"

- "What can you tell me about why we're not quite ready to take this step?"
- "What would need to be in place for you to move forward with this recommendation?"

Keep asking additional questions until you uncover the reasons for the no, and then ask again for a commitment to take steps toward getting what you know needs to be done. This can sound something like this: "So it sounds like the reason you're not ready to move forward with my recommendation is [restate reason]. Assuming we can work through that, could you commit to [the original request]?"

Facilitate

Your role as the buying coach is to recommend, get your champion (and other stakeholders) to commit, and then to facilitate their success in any way possible. Remember that an important part of buyer enablement is about helping the buyers take action. One aspect of this facilitation is helping the champion understand the process and work with the buyer map to engage the right stakeholders at the right time.

Another aspect can be related to the *Equip* stage of the buyer enablement framework. Facilitation could mean equipping the buyer with key pieces of information, content, or job aids. As a simple example, if you know they will almost always receive the same objections from the IT department about general data protection regulation (GDPR) privacy laws and data security, equip them with prepared content to overcome that objection, and then coach them on what to say and do when the concerns come up.

Examples of job aids or toolkits that can help facilitate might include:

- GDPR and other security and privacy compliance docs
- Financial ROI spreadsheets

- Implementation project guides and templates
- Interactive product demos

Another aspect of facilitating might mean getting on the phone with another stakeholder to back up your champion. It might mean bringing in other experts from your side, such as a client success manager or sales engineer. The bottom line is to be there as a resource and try to anticipate what they will need, and provide anything that is necessary to help them.

WORKING WITH A CHAMPION ON BUYER MISALIGNMENT AND DEAL RISK

One of the most useful tools that you can use with a champion is a "buying group alignment analysis" (see Chapter 13, "Measuring Buyer Enablement"). The table captures how much each person in the buying group is persuaded toward or against your solution. Developing the table and showing it to a champion is a great way to coach them in strategizing for steps needed to get more stakeholders on board with your solution. By weighting the results, you can also use alignment maps to help forecast the risk that a deal won't close.

Be Respectfully Confrontational

Ric Charlesworth, the award-winning Australian hockey coach, famously said, "The interesting thing about coaching is that you have to trouble the comfortable, and comfort the troubled."[3] Why do

---

3   Liz Hanson, "Ric Charlesworth–Lessons from an Olympic Coaching Great," Athlete Assessments, https://athleteassessments.com/ric-charlesworth-olympic-coaching/.

coaches have to trouble the comfortable? Because without challenging them, the player risks not reaching his or her potential and ultimately risks not having the capacity to win.

To help your prospect's organization make the leap forward that you know they can make with your solution, you have to be confrontational. Without some tactful confrontation, the buying group is likely to rely on the status quo as the default because it is the least risky. Or, because of perceived risk, they may just decide to go with a well-known alternative that is not in their best interest.

Being the buying coach requires that you challenge the status quo. Ask the tough questions and require your prospects to consider what happens if they don't change it. In the buyer enablement model, this takes a few different forms:

- Asking your champion to step up to the plate on his or her commitments

- Following up with questions such as, "If you don't mind my asking, what got in the way of getting this task done?"

These commitments are key to moving the decision-making process forward, and you can't do it without your champions.

Being respectfully confrontational can also take the form of asking hard questions or insisting that key stakeholders have to be involved. In the end, it is your job to make them extremely uncomfortable with the status quo. Otherwise, there is no reason to change. The more uncomfortable you can make them with their current situation, the more likely they are to make the effort required to change.

After Every Commitment, Reassure

Ric Charlesworth said a good coach has to also "comfort the troubled." When your champion commits, they are essentially saying, "I think it's worth it to take this step. I've assessed the risks and the potential opportunity, and I think the risks are worth taking." Every commitment, and more importantly the follow-through, is a strong buying signal. To help facilitate the follow-through, provide emotional encouragement.

After every commitment, it's important to issue a sincere statement of reassurance and conviction that they've made the right decision. Suppose you just secured a commitment from your champion to share some important materials with her boss. Here's an example of what that might sound like: "Janet, thank you for agreeing to share these materials with your boss and to collect any questions they may have. This is going to make a big difference. Having your boss's support will not only help move this purchasing decision forward but will also make all of the difference when it comes to actually implementing the solution." Reassuring them after the commitment not only keeps everyone feeling positive but also makes it more likely they will follow through.

Making the Hard Calls

I worked with an otherwise stellar salesperson who had a weekly meeting for 30 minutes for over a year with someone who said they were a champion. Week after week there was no progress. Week after week he would get verbal commitments from the supposed champion to getting their tasks done; the rep even began asking if this person would get them done by specific dates. Week after week the dates would go by and nothing would happen. Here and there the prospect made a little movement, just enough to keep my salesperson, who really wanted this deal, on the hook.

Why did my salesperson put up with that? I believe because of two things. First, he wanted the deal so badly that he wasn't willing to admit defeat. John Madden, the famous American football coach, said, "Coaches have to watch for what they don't want to see and listen to what they don't want to hear." As a buying coach, you need to do the same.

The second reason my salesperson kept having this unproductive meeting for over a year was that he was too nice, unwilling to require the champion perform or be "off the team."

Bill Walsh, another American football coach, said this about the difficulty of making the tough decisions:

The [best] coaches . . . know that the job is to win . . . I have spent many sleepless nights trying to figure out how I was going to phase out certain players for whom I had strong feelings, but that was my job. I wasn't hired to do anything but win.[4]

Remember, you were hired to win and nothing else. If the champion isn't getting you where you need to go, just acknowledge that they aren't your champion and you have to recruit another one, maybe even inside another organization.

You're the buying coach. You get to decide who is on your team and who isn't. The better the players (champions) you have on your team, the more deals you get done, and the faster they get done.

---

4   Richard Rapaport, "To Build a Winning Team: An Interview with Head Coach Bill Walsh," *Harvard Business Review*, January–February 1993, https://hbr.org/1993/01/to-build-a-winning-team-an-interview-with-head-coach-bill-walsh.

CHAPTER 11

CONTINUE CHAMPION ENABLEMENT
AFTER THE PURCHASE

"Many will say they are loyal friends, but who can find one
who is truly reliable?"

—PROVERBS 20:6

Many B2B companies, from SaaS to professional services, now employ
a subscription pricing model. This means that getting the deal done
happens every subscription period, not just once. So buyer enablement needs to continue past the purchase to begin the cycle of closing
the next deal: the renewal.

What plagues all B2B SaaS businesses (or any business that
employs a subscription model) is the fact that however good they are
at getting the deal done in the first place, poor implementation and
adoption can destroy their business model altogether.

Many SaaS companies, for example, have a cost of customer acquisition that exceeds the price of the first year's subscription. In other
words, they aren't making money until year two and beyond. In subscription models, gaining the renewal is not only desirable but also
essential for survival. And if you work for a company that employs a

subscription model, it's likely some of your compensation comes from what happens after the sale.

That's why DEEP-C thinking doesn't stop when the purchase is complete. Just as you took the lead in the buying process, you should also take the lead here by thinking about the buyer's post-purchase experience before the ink is dry. The process of applying DEEP-C post-sale is very similar to presale, but keep in mind that the buying group may change significantly over the course of the subscription period.

Identify and Engage Your Champion . . . Again

For starters, the champion for the renewal may be an entirely different person than the original champion. In fact, you may have no champion. Post-sale, sometimes the champion hands off the implementation to a subordinate—sometimes quite abruptly. So your first job is to identify the new champion. Hopefully, this is the person who led the buying group in the first place. If so, you're in luck, and you don't have to try to develop or discover a new champion.

If this is not the case, you'll need to quickly determine who is assigned to be the new leader and if they indeed are your champion post-sale. Quite often, if the purchase is the boss's initiative, they'll hand off the implementation to a subordinate, that person doesn't want to deal with it, and it languishes and dies. To avoid this, look for someone working for that subordinate who can help. This could be an end user or a middle manager who catches the vision and gets excited. If possible, encourage and develop a small group of end users as champions who can help their peers. And keep in mind that whether you are working with the original champion or someone new, you have to start the engagement process again.

After the purchase, your champion isn't thinking about how to get the renewal. They are thinking about how to implement and adopt. Remember, the champion has a lot on the line. I've met people who have lost their jobs because they advocated for software that didn't get adopted or didn't deliver on its brand promise. So they have a lot of reasons why they need to pay close attention to the implementation.

The challenge is momentum. There is a big buildup during the purchasing process that results in the deal getting signed. Once that is done, it's not uncommon for the champion, who has often sidelined other projects to focus on driving the purchase in the buying group, to get distracted with other projects.

TIP

Try to find a backup champion as well. One thing that leads to post-purchase failure is having one point of contact for implementation and post-purchase ROI and then that contact leaves the company or is promoted into another area of their same organization.

Discover and Engage Your Stakeholders . . . Again

Once you've identified your post-purchase champion, make sure you understand the stakeholders in the renewal "buying group." These are the people using your product or solution. The biggest influencers on the renewal will quite often be the mid- and low-level managers who are using the product. They are often only minimally involved, if at all, in the initial purchase, but you can't afford to think your buying group is the same for the renewal. The voices of these managers and the key influential end users will sound like they have a megaphone when the renewal comes up for consideration. They don't think of themselves as part of a buying group, but indeed they are. In fact, they will influence more revenue than the first buying group. How is that possible? Let's take a look at an example.

Metacortex SaaS Software Subscription

Suppose MetaCortex has an average annual subscription deal size of $20,000. Now suppose the churn rate (the rate at which customers do not renew) is 20%. The formula for calculating the lifetime value of a customer is:

1 / churn rate

This means that the average customer lifetime at MetaCortex is five years (= 1 / 0.20) and that puts the average lifetime value at $100,000.

So while the initial buying group is making a decision that represents $20,000 to you and them, the post-purchase buying group is making a decision that represents $80,000. That is four times the revenue influence when compared to the initial buying group. (This assumes the renewal deal size stays at $20,000; in reality, it could be larger if there are account expansions or price increases.)

So it makes sense to apply buyer enablement principles even more rigorously to the post-purchase buying group. Ironically, in many organizations, while there is a lot of focus on how to get good adoption and implementation in general, little effort and tracking is given to discovering the personas and key players involved in getting the renewal.

Equip and Coach Your Champion . . . Again

Think about implementation and post-purchase value creation as a group activity, just like the first buying process. Companies need to equip and coach the champion post-sale as much or more as during the sale. Buyers want more post-purchase guidance than they currently get from most vendors, including details about integration, potential roadblocks, workforce training, and so on.

Does this mean that it's all on the sales rep? No. This responsibility is quite often placed on the client success team. However, you can help them by sharing buying enablement principles and helping them to form the beginnings of the renewal buying group during the initial buying process.

Just as with the initial buying process, the champion, as well as the client success team, will require coaching. And then the client success team will pick up the equipping and coaching and lead to the renewal. Remember that at the core of buyer enablement is delivering on a content strategy that drives to a successful purchase. This also applies to the renewal.

The kinds of content needed depend on the stakeholders and what they need to implement effectively. That means after the purchase supplying an internal champion with:

- Implementation and adoption guides that walk them through a successful implementation step-by-step
- Case studies that show how other customers implemented successfully
- Promotional materials for internal efforts to promote the changes required to be successful
- End user training options that include on-site training and self-directed e-learning options

At the risk of overstating the obvious, if the champion can lead an effective implementation, they will realize the value your solution provides and be much more likely to renew. Looking at the renewal process through the lens of the DEEP-C framework can help you see areas to improve.

Designate a Program for Champion Enablement

As I began recognizing the tremendous impact on success that buyer enablement was having on the customers whom my company works with, I began predicting that the industry's increasing focus on buyer enablement was inevitably going to lead to new job titles and descriptions in vendors. I imagined a role solely dedicated to providing content and resources to the champion—effectively a champion advocate.

So when I ran across Bimala (Tullock) Rose, who was working for a leading SaaS company and had the title of *Director, Champion Enablement*, I was more than intrigued and reached out to her. She agreed to an interview.

What surprised me most was that she wasn't providing resources to prospects, but she was wholly dedicated to enabling the champion *after* the sale. She sat in the Customer Success department.

Of course, the lights went on immediately. While almost all of my research and experience had been focused on getting the purchase to happen, Bimala's Champion Enablement program's focus was entirely on driving value and expansion and securing the renewal by equipping the post-purchase champion. She focused on providing champions with a digital portal stocked with self-service guides and templates for accelerating value from the purchased platform and buy-in from users.

"We've established a 'self-help' portal all customers have access to, with no additional charge. Customers don't need to make a request to gain access or even have a purchase threshold. The materials walk them through a simple process on how to execute, and provide templates to get them started," Bimala told me.

These guides and templates available through the portal cover the following topics:

- The steps to drive adoption of the new technology prior, during, and after go-live

- A framework to design and implement a program that drives continued value from the platform, including team structure

- How to engage with other departments to communicate the value the platform could bring to their departments

The Champion Enablement program's interactions yielded tremendous success, with reports showing that clients who accessed the materials were adopting faster and expanding more successfully than customers who had not accessed the materials.

While a focus on customer success with an emphasis on obtaining the renewal is nothing new, Bimala's Champion Enablement strategy was to concentrate on enabling and partnering with the customer champion to more effectively drive expansion and renewal. Your company may want to follow this example and designate someone to build a Champion Enablement program as well.

You're Still in Charge of Buying, Temporarily

As the salesperson or sales leader, you'll need not only to get the deal done but also to set up the deal to have a good chance at getting a great renewal. Hopefully your compensation incentivizes you to do this; if not, for the good of the company's health, this is still your role.

You need to start forming the renewal buying group during the sales process. This means that you are coaching your champion to identify who will be implementing the software. What teams? What users specifically? When? Begin to form a relationship with these other stakeholders and introduce them to the client success team *before* the deal gets done. Again, it's imperative this work begins *before* because after the purchase is complete, momentum dies off quickly.

PART III

GETTING STARTED WITH BUYER ENABLEMENT:
THE TECHNOLOGIES AND METHODS FOR EFFECTIVE BUYER ENABLEMENT IMPLEMENTATION

CHAPTER 12

FORGING A PATH

"To learn and not to do is really not to learn. To know and not to do
is really not to know."

—STEPHEN COVEY[1]

I hope by now that I've convinced you that buyer enablement is a strategy and technology that can benefit you and your buyers. But just having that knowledge isn't enough. You must put what you know into practice before the knowledge will make any difference. If we don't "do," then our lives continue as if we never learned in the first place.

As of the writing of this book, however, there is a major challenge with "doing" when it comes to buyer enablement: There is no single methodology or technology that encompasses all of the functionalities that you need. So you will have to decide what elements of buyer enablement you want to implement, and pull together a solution composed of different methods and technologies tailored to your buyers' needs. Let's take a quick look at the overall process for developing content needed to better equip your champion to sell, and then look at technology components that may come into the picture if you want to up your game.

---

1   Stephen R. Covey, *The Seven Habits of Highly Effective People* (New York: Free Press, 1989): 12.

Just Do It

How you start is important. Many strategies for improvement fail from the outset not because the strategy or change is flawed but because the effort to implement the change is so broad and heavy that it never gets off the ground.

Have you heard the Winston Churchill quote, "Perfection is the enemy of progress"? The concept has been promoted for centuries.[2] Consider these quotes from sages past:

- Voltaire: "The best is the enemy of the good."

- Confucius: "Better a diamond with a flaw than a pebble without."

- Shakespeare: "Striving to better, oft we mar what's well."

Everything I've ever accomplished, including writing this book, has required putting my desire to deliver perfection to the side and get the first version done—and then improve on it. That's why my first piece of advice for implementing buyer enablement and the DEEP-C framework is to start small, don't wait, and set your sights on an imperfect first version.

If you're a sales leader, pick a product, a single segment, and a team to begin testing the buyer enablement approach and the DEEP-C framework in the reality of your team's daily life. If you get good results, do more and broaden the experiment. If you continue to get good results, go all in.

If you're a sales professional, follow the steps in the following guide on your own, and your buyers will be closing more deals for you sooner than you realize.

---

2   See these two excellent articles on the subject: Neil Patel, "Your Secret Mental Weapon: 'Don't Let the Perfect Be the Enemy of the Good,'" *Entrepreneur*, August 31, 2015, https://www.entrepreneur.com/article/249676, and Deep Patel, "Why Perfection Is the Enemy of Done," *Forbes*, June 16, 2017, https://www.forbes.com/sites /deeppatel/2017/06/16/why-perfection-is-the-enemy-of-done/#126d49b94395.

Quick Start Guide to Launching a DEEP-C Buyer Enablement Effort

Here are my recommended steps to get started. Don't consider them the gospel truth. Instead, consider them a guide to get started quickly, and then adjust as you go.

As you can see, there are three basic phases: putting together a project team, describing the typical buying group, and then developing and leveraging content specific to different members of the buying group. Here, I detail key steps within these phases; most of them pertain to all implementations of buyer enablement, whether or not you use technology.

Phase I: Establish a buyer enablement team

- If not yourself, recruit someone on your team to lead the DEEP-C cause.

- Decide on pilot product, target segment, and a team of sales professionals.

- Define metrics you want to track.

- Train the team on buyer enablement fundamentals, including the components of DEEP-C and the need to focus on identifying all the members of typical buying groups for your solutions and then equipping internal champions to sell to those stakeholders.

TIP

You will likely have different buying group personas and tasks for different segments, product lines, or industries. So make sure to start with a rather narrow target for the pilot so the planning doesn't get out of hand.

Phase II: Describe a typical buying group

- Analyze previous successful deals, and map out the buyer personas, the stages they enter the buying process, who the typical champion is, and common questions and concerns for each buyer persona as they relate to the targets of the pilot. Consider organizing the content around buyer issues (described in the next section of this chapter).
- Create a one-sheet for each persona on the buying group, intended for the champion, that includes:
  - Profile
  - Common role in the buying process
  - Common questions and concerns
  - Tasks that role is usually responsible for completing to get the purchase done
  - Content or answers to help the champion with that question or concern
- Map out the typical buying process—this includes the tasks and steps the buying group has to go through to successfully get the deal done.

Phase III: Develop content and implement as you go

- Explore what resources you currently have for buyers that match up to the different questions and tasks in the buying process and buying group. Determine the content gap. Analyze existing content to see if there is content for each question or concern.
- Create a project plan to fill the content gaps so that, where possible, you have content to address the needs of each stakeholder.
- Start building the content.

- Use it as you build it. Don't wait. Begin equipping your champions with that content as they drive the deal inside. I recommend organizing your buyer enablement content by stage during the purchasing process so that your sales team is more likely to deliver content to the champion that is relevant to the tasks the buyers are dealing with at the time.

- If possible, use software that is designed to enable buyers and that helps you discover and engage the buying group by personalizing content for each stakeholder. (I'll go into technology capabilities later in this chapter in more detail.)

- Continue to complete the content plan as you go until you have a complete set of content pieces mapped to the needs of every buyer persona at every stage of the buying process.

Of all these steps, the most critical in terms of fulfilling the buyer enablement promise—providing the right content to the right stakeholder at the right time—are those that deal with identifying the buying personas you typically encounter and having content relevant to the stakeholders who fill those personas.

Content Priorities: What Will Help Your Champions Sell More Effectively?

The ultimate goal in buyer enablement is to provide content that speaks directly to the needs of each prospect's industry, company, and stakeholder roles. This isn't easy—remember any given B2B buying group could have five to nine stakeholders involved, and perhaps even more. If you want every one of them to be on board and in support of your solution, then you have to personalize the experience to each stakeholder. Just as a rep in a live demo can adjust their approach on the fly based on new information from each stakeholder, your reps (and software, if you use it) need to be able to adjust as well.

Keep in mind that it's important not to overwhelm the buyer with information. As you make information accessible online, make sure that there are mechanisms in place for them to easily get at the information they need for that stage in the buyer journey.

In other words, don't try to answer every question that the buyers might have with content. In-depth queries can be handled during live sales interactions. Instead, weigh and prioritize the types of questions that buyers have most often, and use the 80/20 rule to develop content that will answer the 20% of the questions that will have 80% of the impact on the buying decision.

This is key to buyer enablement. Too often, I see salespeople and teams creating online deal and data rooms full of information that leave buyers lost in a maze of information, unsure about where to go to find the right information for their stage in the buying journey and for their role in the buying group.

It's not about the quantity of the information but rather the right amount of information at the right time for the right stakeholder.

To help you do that, keep in mind that every stakeholder that joins the buying group has questions they need answered and tasks they are either influencing or need to complete. Instead of making a list of important topics or important tasks, look at the map of your typical buying groups and list the questions that need answers and the tasks that need to be completed.

Gartner's approach to organizing content centers around three activity streams: Explore (Why?), Evaluate (What?), and Engage (How?).[3] Figure 31 shows their Example Content Asset Map.

---

3   Gartner, Accelerate Buying Decisions Through a Customer Centric 'Questions to Answer' Content Strategy, *Hank Barnes, Michael Maziarka*, November 22, 2019.

Activity Stream	Core Questions to Answer	Roles Addressed	Content Assets
Explore (Why?)	Question 1	Executive, business unit (BU), IT	Content Asset 1
	Question 2	Executive, BU, IT	Content Asset 2
Evaluate (What?)	Question 3	BU, IT	Content Asset 3
	Question 4	BU	Content Asset 4
Engage (How?)	Question 5	BU, IT	Content Asset 5
	Question 6	IT	Content Asset 6

Source: Gartner (November 2019)

Figure 31: Gartner's "Example Content Asset Map." I recommend using a table like this to help sales reps keep track of which pieces of content are available on demand to meet the needs of which specific personas in a buying group.

Those three activity streams from Gartner's research are just the beginning and relate to product marketing. For the purpose of sales, I recommend that you continue to map content through vendor selection and execution (implementation).

The actions your buyers need to take may be unique to your buying journey. The best source is to look at closed deals and ask, "What are the actions the buyers need to complete to get the deal done?" Then follow it up with "How can we facilitate each action to make it easier or more pleasant?" Remember, the goal in buyer enablement is to make purchasing easier for the buyer.

Technology Capabilities to Consider

Educating yourself and your reps about buyer enablement will generate immediate impact; focusing on what your buyers need at every step of their purchasing process will make you a better salesperson and help your champions do a better job for you even before you implement any technology. But once you start implementing a buyer-focused mentality, it quickly becomes clear that the results are limited in terms of speed and closing rates unless you leverage supporting technology.

Because there is no existing comprehensive solution for implementing buyer enablement, you should look for key software categories and feature sets that support buyer enablement. There are three main categories of software that are most helpful in supporting buyer enablement:

Intelligent Demo Automation Software

Demos are an essential part of educating the buying group. You can tailor live demos to each stakeholder, but this stretches out the sales cycle, and the experience is inconsistent from rep to rep. An interactive demo automation platform allows you to put your sales process in overdrive. It will help scale your sales, increase sales productivity, shorten the sales cycle, and decrease the cost of customer acquisition—all while delivering incredible customer insights through analytics (See chapters 14 and 15 for more information on demo automation).

ROI Analysis Software

At some point, every buying group has to decide if the financials make sense. ROI analysis software delivers an online ROI calculation, sometimes put together in tandem with the rep and sometimes self-directed. If designed effectively, this type of software will also deliver key analytics about the ROI assumptions of different stakeholders.

Social Proof Software

Buyers don't want to be the first one to take the risk. Social proof software should offer self-directed ways for the buying group to access case studies, customer testimonials and videos, and even facilitate reference requests.

When purchasing buyer enablement software, consider that the most effective buyer enablement platforms have the following feature sets:

- Engage through automated discovery
- Make the content easy to share with other stakeholders
- Track organic stakeholder discovery
- Tailor the experience to each buyer's interests and needs (deep personalization)
- Collect data that can be used to analyze patterns and misalignment
- Provide notifications and dashboards for the sales team and the internal champion(s)
- Offers plug-ins to existing technology
- Facilitate communication between the buying group and the sales team

You'll find many of these capabilities in some sales tech stack tools, but it's rare to find all of them in any given tool. Let's review each one and see what it brings to the picture.

ANOTHER FUNCTIONALITY: ANYTIME, ANYWHERE ACCESS

Salespeople won't want to use buyer enablement software unless it is easy to use. Make sure the technology you choose is available for the salespeople to use via email and CRM integrations, as well as via mobile devices.

Capability 1: Engage Through Automated Discovery

The only way to educate buyers about your solution in a way that is most relevant to them is to ask questions that will reveal how you need to personalize what you teach them. That's true whether you're using actual people delivering a live demo or technology to fill that role. In short, the discovery process that reps go through in live demos by asking questions should be imitated with the software. Look for software that asks questions of every stakeholder or lets each stakeholder rate levels of interest, then sends those responses back to the sales team and to the internal champion.

Capability 2: Make the Content Easy to Share with Other Stakeholders

Buyer enablement software should make it easy for your champion to share your videos and documents with other stakeholders. Look for software that employs multiple methods for sharing, as well as prompts your prospects to share. When the prospect begins to share, they begin to advocate, and you're on your way to pulling the buying group together faster than ever before.

Capability 3: Track Organic Stakeholder Discovery

Key to buyer enablement is discovering and engaging different stakeholders as early as possible. Your buyer enablement software should track which people are engaging and how their engagement is the same as or different from other stakeholders in the buying group. As a bonus, it should give your stakeholders titles and contact information where possible. (Note: In Europe, data protection laws such as GDPR may sometimes reduce this benefit.)

Capability 4: Tailor the Experience to Each Buyer's Interests and Needs (Deep Personalization)

What are you going to do with the information you put in your buyer enablement plan? The answer should be obvious by now: Personalize the experience to each stakeholder. No stakeholder in the buying group wants to engage with content that isn't relevant to them.

What does "personalization" mean? There is a lot of hype about personalizing video and other content to prospects. Much of the time "personalized video" means the vendor is able to insert a logo or the person's name in the video. While nifty and somewhat useful at catching their attention, do not mistake this superficial personalization for the kind of personalization that will have a true impact.

Research shows that buyers not only want digital access to information that is on-demand but also still expect "a tailored experience relevant to their interests and needs"[4]—what I call "deep personalization." So when you organize your digital content strategy for your sales team to enable the buyers, make sure to base it on technology that can personalize the content on the fly to the unique interests of each stakeholder in the buying group. The buyer enablement software must be able to analyze the responses to key discovery questions and actually change the content to tailor it to each stakeholder's unique interests and needs.

For example, the end user is going to want to see different parts of your solution than management will. Maybe management cares most about reporting and analytics, and the end user cares most about getting the job done. Your software needs to be able to adapt to these different needs—just as a sales rep would hold separate meetings with these stakeholders and adapt their message for each audience.

---

4   "2017 B2B Buyers Survey Report," Demand Gen,
    https://www.demandgenreport.com/resources/research/2017-b2b-buyers-survey-report.

Capability 5: Collect Data That Can Be Used to Analyze Patterns and Misalignment

The next chapter explains the kinds of analyses that help get the most out of your buyer enablement efforts. Obviously, you can't do any kinds of analysis unless you have information and data to start with. So through manual or automatic means (or most likely a combination of both), you need to be able to tell whether a champion has been identified, how many of the stakeholders discovered represent the various personas in the buying group, how many of them have engaged and to what extent, and so on. Most importantly, you need to collect data that will allow you to analyze each stakeholder's primary interests and their engagement in the context of all other stakeholders so you and your champion can quickly see alignment or misalignment.

Whether or not you end up purchasing software that supports buyer enablement, you can take steps to move in the right direction by adapting your existing customer relations management (CRM) technology. Most CRMs allow you to build out custom stages and custom fields in deals in play. I highly recommend using your CRM to track some (maybe even many) aspects of buyer enablement. You might consider adding these custom fields to the opportunity record in Salesforce or whatever CRM you are using:

- Champion Identified (Y/N)
- Stakeholder persona name fields (you'll need a separate contact field for each persona in the buying group; the account executive must select the contact that fits that persona slot)
- Stakeholder persona "Engaged" and "Approves" fields (Y/N) (place these next to the persona contact name field.)
- Buyer Enablement jobs (with my recommended wording):
  - Problem identified
  - Solution decided
  - Validation
  - Consensus achieved

Capability 6: Provide Notifications and Dashboards for the Sales Team and the Internal Champion(s)

As I mentioned earlier, buyer enablement technology should allow you to provide not only personalized information (when and how each different buyer wants it) but also what gives you *and your champion(s)* a bigger window into what's going on in terms of persuading the buying group to support your solution. That means you want technology that can notify you and the champion about progress in the buying process.

There is a lot of software out there that will notify the person who sent the content when a recipient clicks the link, looks at the email, or looks at a piece of content. What is often missing from this process is notifying all of the parties that need to know. For example, you and other members of your sales team need to know when your champion and other stakeholders engage with your automated demo or other content.

"You need to make sure different contacts within the selling organization are joined at the hip," says Paul Norris, former VP of global solution architecture at CA Technologies. "On large deals, loan them a dedicated SE (Sales Engineer). Get Professional Services involved. Engage an internal architect or subject matter expert about the business problem. Remember, there is a 'Selling Group' too!"[5]

Today, B2B sales is a team-based activity. Early in the sales cycle, you have business development representatives and account executives that need to coordinate. Later you have account executives and sales engineers, client success, and professional services that need to coordinate.

If the business development representative sends out an automated demo, for example, both the business development representative and the account executive should be notified when they engage so they can look at the analytics.

Just notifying your sales team, however, isn't enough. Remember, your goal is to better equip your champions to sell for you. Yet most software designed for traditional sales enablement assumes only the sales team needs to know which stakeholders are engaging and when.

---

5 Paul Norris, in discussion with the author, January 26, 2018.

Champions cannot be fully enabled if they are kept in the dark about what is happening with demos, content, and so on. So make sure your buyer enablement software includes both a dashboard and notifications that allow the champion to know who and when their colleagues are engaging.

Capability 7: Offer Plug-ins to Existing Technology

Salespeople won't want to use buyer enablement software unless it is easy to use. Make sure the technology you choose is available for the salespeople to use via email and CRM integrations, as well as via mobile devices.

Capability 8: Facilitate Communication Between the Buying Group and the Sales Team

One way you need to make buying easier is to make it easier for the buyers to communicate with the sales team. On the sales side, there are often multiple people involved (such as sales development rep, account executive, sales engineer, finance, and so on). Given that a dozen or more stakeholders usually get involved on the buyer side and at least three to five people on the vendor side, there are often ten to fifteen people trying to engage at one point or another to get the purchase done.

Less-experienced salespeople often resort to email, phone calls, and meetings. Better salespeople build a relationship and use text messaging to move conversations more quickly. The best salespeople who truly understand the need to facilitate the buying group are setting up deal chat channels on technologies such as Slack or Zoom.

Look for technologies that make it easy for the buying group to ask questions of different members of the vendor team and to other stakeholders within the buying group. The bottom line is that the easier it is, the more often and faster communication happens and the faster the purchasing decision gets made.

Prepping Your Reps

Buyer enablement is not only about personalized content at the right place at the right time; it's also about bringing the buying group together and coaching the champion(s) effectively. I recommend the following steps for helping your reps get oriented and off on the right foot.

Download the Buyer Enablement Sales Training Deck for some useful assets to help you get started at the following link: buyerenablement.io

Discover the Champion and Stakeholders

Train your reps on what a real champion is. Too often, inexperienced reps think they have a great champion because someone loves their solution. But remember, that person isn't a champion until they start taking the risks necessary to advocate and bring the buying group together. As a follow-up to your training, begin asking your reps who the champion is and what actions those people have taken to demonstrate that they are real champions.

Make sure to train your reps on the buying group map you've devised and the different personas. Role-play how to discover stakeholders, and if you are using technology that supports buyer enablement, give them guidelines on how you want them to use it in their daily workflow.

Become Better Coaches

Helping your reps become better coaches is perhaps the hardest challenge of all. I recommend role-playing for several weeks. If your reps begin with the simple steps of recommending, asking for commitments, and helping the champion be successful at delivering on their commitments, you'll start to see immediate impact. Practice and review with them for several weeks, and it will become a habit that will drive success over the long term.

Start Measuring and Behavior Will Follow

No amount of preaching and persuading can replace the simple act of beginning to measure actions and process outcomes. If you begin tracking the number of stakeholders or asking, "Which of the stakeholders in the buying group map are engaged on this deal?" your reps will respond even if they haven't responded before.

Don't Wait to Get Started

Remember: Start small, don't wait, and set your sights on an imperfect first version.

Adopting the mindset of knowing that buyers do most of your selling is a major shift for most salespeople. You and your sales team won't know everything that you need to know up front, but don't let that stop you. Develop content and methods based on prior experience, and then make sure you have mechanisms in place to *learn* as you go—so the next version can be better than the last. This way, you'll be able to reap the gains of buyer enablement sooner rather than later.

CHAPTER 13

MEASURING BUYER ENABLEMENT

"If you don't collect any metrics, you're flying blind. If you collect and focus on too many, they may be obstructing your field of view."

—SCOTT M. GRAFFIUS, *AGILE SCRUM*[1]

By now, the value proposition of buyer enablement should be quite clear: higher close rates and shorter sales cycles. Tracking those two high-level outcome metrics is therefore a given. But there are many other process metrics that can help you (and the champion) determine mid-stream how well a deal is progressing and what else remains to help your buyers make the purchase decision.

Some of this data has to be generated manually—having sales reps enter information in your CRM or buyer enablement software—but some should be generated automatically by your software.

---

1 Scott M. Graffius, "'Agile Scrum: Your Quick-Start Guide with Step-by-Step Instructions' Quoted in 'Innovation Management,'" Scott M. Graffius, blog, November 23, 2018, https://www.scottgraffius.com/blog/files/tag-201cif-you-don2019t-collect-any -metrics002c-you2019re-flying-blind.201d.html.

Basic Data for Buyer Enablement

There are eight kinds of data that I think are most useful in helping to track how well you are enabling your buyers:

1. Champion(s) identified

2. Number of stakeholders discovered

3. Prioritized interests of the buying group

4. Percentage of buying group discovered

5. Percentage of buying group engaged

6. Percentage of buying group showing approval

7. Share rate

8. Buying stages each stakeholder has completed

Some of these items, like whether a champion is identified, can be determined by adding yes or no or checkbox fields to your CRM or other records. Other data points, especially those that deal with tracking or sharing (metrics 5, 7, and 8, in particular) are nearly impossible to determine by traditional means and must involve software that can do the tracking for you. Let's look at each of these metrics in more detail.

Champion(s) Identified

The first key question for any buying coach (note, I'm not calling them a "sales rep") should be, "Have I identified a champion?" As I've discussed throughout, without an internal champion, it's almost impossible to get a deal done.

Also, you may have multiple champions working in tandem to help drive the solution. So when you build this metric out in your CRM, make sure that reps have the ability to assign the "champion" designation to any contact associated with the opportunity.

Individual reps or management may find it helpful to compile a table or CRM report like that shown in Table B as a way to track this key information across multiple deals.

TABLE C: CHAMPIONS IDENTIFIED

Deal #	Deal Name	At least one champion identified?
1	Aardvark	Yes
2	Bear	Yes
3	Cheetah	No
4	Dog	Yes
5	Elephant	No
6	Fox	No
7	Giraffe	Yes
8	Hippo	Yes
Percentage of deals with champions identified:		5/8 = 62.5%

Number of Stakeholders Discovered

Tracking the aggregate number of stakeholders will help your team stay focused on the buying group and the buying perspective, as well as tell you whether or not your team as a whole is starting to adopt this thinking. Tracking the number of stakeholders per deal is a quick indicator of whether or not that deal has enough stakeholders involved to get a purchase decision.

You can track stakeholders manually or speed up the process through technology. The rapid, viral spread of engagement with your self-directed demos and content is a key differentiator of technology-supported buyer enablement. So you want to be able to track how many stakeholders are being discovered and how quickly. There are two numbers that relate to this goal:

Aggregate

Track the raw number of stakeholders discovered across all active deals for a rep or a sales team. Among other purposes, doing so increases

pressure on sales reps: They will want to demonstrate they are con-
tributing to the number and will increase their efforts at discovering
the stakeholders. At the beginning of the buyer enablement effort, the
number of stakeholders discovered will be relatively low, but it should
steadily climb until it levels off and becomes a new status quo target
(see Table D). This type of metric tracking will help you know if you're
getting better as a team at identifying stakeholders.

TABLE D: METRIC 2A—AGGREGATE STAKEHOLDERS
TOTAL NUMBER OF STAKEHOLDERS IDENTIFIED

Deal	May 1	May 15	June 1
Aardvark	1	3	7
Bear	1	2	3
Cheetah	0	2	4
Dog	5	7	7
Elephant	3	7	9
Fox	2	3	6
Giraffe	4	4	5
Hippo	0	3	5
Total	16	31	46

Relative to a specific deal

After analyzing previously won deals, you should have a good sense
of the number of stakeholders involved in deals that close for your
various solutions. So a simple way to know whether or not any particular deal is likely to get done is to look at how many stakeholders are
involved in the deal (see Table E). While not granular, this can help be
a quick gut-check test to know if the sales rep has the right amount of
traction across the buying group. Suppose a sales rep says, "On this
deal, I have an awesome champion who loves our solution, and three
key stakeholders have bought in." Sounds good, doesn't it? But if past

data shows that most deals of that type require five to six stakeholders to close, the deal is in trouble even though a champion is on board. That should prompt the manager to sit down with the rep and take a closer look at what stakeholder personas are missing from the buying group and encourage the rep to proactively get them involved.

TABLE E: METRIC 2B—RELATIVE NUMBER OF STAKEHOLDERS

Opportunity Name	Company	Stakeholders Discovered	Typical Needed	Gap	Risk Assessment
Deal 1	ACME CO	5	8	-3	☹
Deal 2	XYZ Corp	9	8	+1	☺

Prioritized Interests of the Buying Group

Looking at data across an entire group of buyers is one of the most helpful aspects of using buyer enablement software. You should be able to compile the data on individual buyer interests to look at patterns among a buying group. Since you're looking at data across a buying group, you want a table that has a visual indicator about how interested people are in different topics.

Figure 32, for example, shows a sample data from six buying group members about their individual interests. The dark grey indicates *very important*, the light grey *somewhat important*, and the empty circle *not important*. As you can see, the following topics are highly important to the entire buying group:

- Increasing margin
- Building your automated demo
- Dashboards and demolytics (or demo analytics)
- Demos in multiple languages
- Scaling as you move up or down market

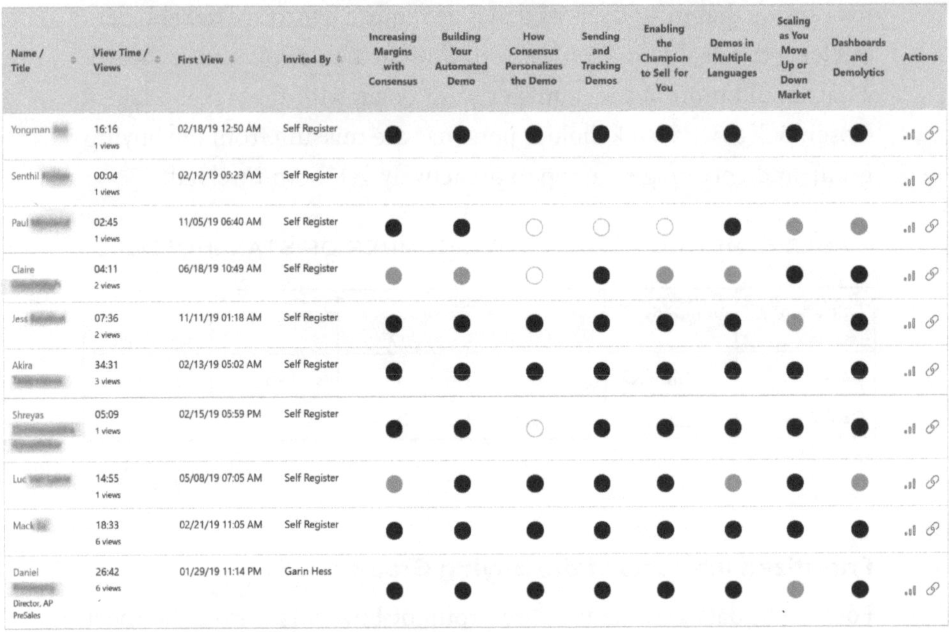

Name / Title	View Time / Views	First View	Invited By	Increasing Margins with Consensus	Building Your Automated Demo	How Consensus Personalizes the Demo	Sending and Tracking Demos	Enabling the Champion to Sell for You	Demos in Multiple Languages	Scaling as You Move Up or Down Market	Dashboards and Demolytics	Actions
Yongman	16:16 1 views	02/18/19 12:50 AM	Self Register	●	●	●	●	●	●	●	●	
Senthil	00:04 1 views	02/12/19 05:23 AM	Self Register									
Paul	02:45 1 views	11/05/19 06:40 AM	Self Register	●	●	○	○	○	●	◍	◍	
Claire	04:11 2 views	06/18/19 10:49 AM	Self Register	◍	◍	○	●	◍	◍	●	●	
Jess	07:36 2 views	11/11/19 01:18 AM	Self Register	●	●	●	●	●	●	◍	●	
Akira	34:31 3 views	02/13/19 05:02 AM	Self Register	●	●	●	●	●	●	●	●	
Shreyas	05:09 1 views	02/15/19 05:59 PM	Self Register	●	●	○	●	●	●	●	●	
Luc	14:55 1 views	05/08/19 07:05 AM	Self Register	◍	●	●	●	●	◍	●	◍	
Mack	18:33 6 views	02/21/19 11:05 AM	Self Register	●	●	●	●	●	●	●	●	
Daniel Director, AP PreSales	26:42 6 views	01/29/19 11:14 PM	Garin Hess	●	●	●	●	●	●	◍	●	

Figure 32: This example from Consensus software shows how a sales team and the champion can track how interested each stakeholder is in the topics they have access to.

When you see topics that are highly important across the group, follow up with questions such as:

- "Why does this topic rank at the top of everyone's importance list?"
- "Can you explain why this is so important to your whole buying group?"

For example, Figure 32 shows that "How Consensus personalizes the demo" ranges from very important to not important to different stakeholders. As a follow-up, one of our buying coaches could ask the champion something like, "I see some of you marked this as very important and some as not important. Why is this topic so important to some of you and not important to others?"

It's especially valuable to help facilitate the conversation about where there might be misalignment, because if you don't, that misalignment might rear its head in ugly ways later in the purchasing process.

At an aggregate level, one purpose for this kind of data is to make sure that you're providing the right information to your buyers. For example, if there are topics that no one is highly interested in viewing, then you've missed the mark in terms of the types of issues you address. Another purpose is helping you and your champion understand what is truly important to the buying group. While the enablement software is charged with meeting those priority needs, your sales team and champions can use the list as a check to ensure your approach is on track.

Percentage of Buying Group Discovered

This metric is critical for deal review and is similar to the Number of Stakeholders Discovered metric, but it looks at the percentage of stakeholders discovered in any given deal relative to the average number of personas across multiple deals of the same type.

A common mistake when trying to track this metric is to add up the total number of stakeholders discovered and divide by the total number of stakeholders needed to close all deals. The problem with this approach is that you might have many stakeholders on one deal and many fewer than you need on other deals, but in aggregate it could look like you have all that you need.

For example, if your average to close a deal is six stakeholders, and you are analyzing five deals and one of the deals has twelve stakeholders, three others have six, and that last deal has one stakeholder, you would end up with >100% (31/30). So you might think you're doing great, when in reality one of your deals is not even close to having the right number.

Table F shows a simple but misleading way to analyze the percentage of stakeholder involvement. G shows a better way, which gives you a more realistic picture.

TABLE F: THE WRONG WAY TO ANALYZE
STAKEHOLDER DISCOVERY

Deal Name	Company	Total of Stakeholders Discovered	Number of Stakeholders Needed	Percentage of Stakeholders Discovered
Deal 1	Company 1	6	6	100%
Deal 2	Company 2	12	6	200%
Deal 3	Company 3	6	6	100%
Deal 4	Company 4	1	6	16%
Deal 5	Company 5	6	6	100%
Total		31	30	103%

TABLE G: A BETTER WAY TO ANALYZE
STAKEHOLDER DISCOVERY

Deal Name	Total Stakeholders Discovered	Number of Relevant Stakeholders Discovered	Number of Stakeholders Needed	Percentage of Relevant Stakeholders Discovered
Deal 1	6	6	6	100%
Deal 2	12	6	6	100%
Deal 3	6	6	6	100%
Deal 4	1	1	6	16%
Deal 5	6	6	6	100%
Total Relevant Stakeholders	31	25	30	83%

In Table G, notice that I put in the word "relevant" in the number of stakeholders column. That's because for the purpose of evaluating, only the first six are relevant. The others are not relevant to the overall metric. In this table, the 83% of stakeholders discovered is a better reflection on the reality of the situation. Four of the five deals appear to be in good shape. One is definitely not.

Let's take this a step further. Just acquiring sufficient random stakeholders isn't enough. You need to fill the stakeholder persona slots that you've identified as key to getting deals done. For example, if you're selling into the sales team and typically you need six stakeholders involved to get the deal done, but the only stakeholders you have involved so far are low-level sales representatives and no sales leadership roles are involved, clearly the number of stakeholders, as a single metric, does not reflect the likelihood to close.

To calculate this metric effectively, each rep needs to be identifying the stakeholder *personas* that they've discovered. Say, for example, that you know the average number of stakeholder personas needed to close a deal is six. If a rep says they have five stakeholders already identified, it makes a big difference whether those five represent five of the six different personas or only two or three. That's why tracking the percentage of the personas who have been linked to specific individuals is critical in being able to evaluate the true status of a deal. To determine this number:

- Calculate the percentage per deal by using this formula: number of stakeholder personas discovered per deal/number of target stakeholder personas.

- Average the results on all open deals.

Table H shows the same table as F but instead focuses on whether or not we have at least one stakeholder who meets the required persona slot in the typical buying group.

TABLE H: ANALYZING PERSONA DISCOVERY

Deal Name	Total Stakeholders Discovered	Number of Relevant Personas Discovered	Number of Personas Needed	Percentage of Stakeholders Discovered
Deal 1	6	6	6	100%
Deal 2	12	4	6	66%
Deal 3	6	3	6	50%
Deal 4	1	1	6	16%
Deal 5	6	2	6	33%
Total Relevant Stakeholders	31	16	30	53%

Now we see the truth begin to emerge. Out of the 31 stakeholders across these five deals that have been discovered, only 16 fill the slots of the various personas needed to get the deals done. This means that we're only 53% of the way there and that there is high risk among several of the deals, especially deals 3, 4, and 5.

Percentage of Buying Group Engaged

This metric is very similar to metric four (Percentage of Buying Group Discovered) except you need to know whether a stakeholder is not just *discovered* but actually *engaged*—meaning that the person has interacted with some of the content provided through buyer enablement technology or met with the rep personally.

The arithmetic for this metric is:

- Determine the size of the buying group for a particular deal.
- Divide by the number of relevant persona-based stakeholders who have engaged with the content or the rep.

You can combine metrics four and five in a single report that looks something like Table I.

TABLE I: PERCENTAGE OF BUYING GROUP ENGAGED

Deal Name	Total Stakeholders Discovered	Number of Relevant Personas Discovered	Number of Relevant Personas Engaged	Number of Personas Needed	Percentage of Relevant Stakeholders Discovered	Percentage of Relevant Stakeholders Engaged
Deal 1	6	6	4	6	100%	80%
Deal 2	12	4	3	6	100%	50%
Deal 3	6	3	3	6	50%	50%
Deal 4	1	1	1	6	16%	16%
Deal 5	6	2	2	6	33%	33%
Total Relevant Stakeholders	31	16	13	30	53%	43%

This metric paints an even more challenging, but more truthful, picture of the deals in progress. Only 43% of the stakeholders needed are engaged. Even deal 1, which has all of the stakeholders needed already discovered, has more risk than we saw in the previous table because two of them are not engaged.

Percentage of Buying Group Showing Approval

This percentage is similar to the previous two metrics except you're focused on what percentage of a buying group is leaning strongly positively toward your solution. This tracks the alignment across the buying group. To get to this metric, the sales rep will need to manually enter data in your CRM or other software to indicate which personas have bought in and which haven't, and then the CRM report should calculate an overall percentage of stakeholders who support your solution (Table J).

TABLE J: BUYING GROUP APPROVAL ANALYSIS

Deal Name	Total Stakeholders Discovered	Number of Relevant Personas Discovered	Number of Relevant Personas Engaged	Number of Relevant Personas Showing Approval	Number of Personas Needed	Percentage of Relevant Stakeholders Discovered	Percentage of Relevant Stakeholders Engaged	Percentage of Buying Group Showing Approval
Deal 1	6	6	4	3	6	100%	80%	50%
Deal 2	12	4	3	3	6	100%	50%	50%
Deal 3	6	3	3	2	6	50%	50%	50%
Deal 4	1	1	1	0	6	16%	16%	0%
Deal 5	6	2	2	2	6	33%	33%	33%
Total Relevant Stakeholders	31 (stake-holders discovered)	16 (relevant personas)	13 (relevant personas)	10 (relevant personas)	30	53%	43%	33%

Now we begin to see a real picture of how far along the buying groups are. We're only about one-third of the way there overall with these five deals. This is a much better way to do quick deal review than based on the sales process stage indicated by the sales rep. The current way of doing deal review based on stages of the sales cycle shows too many false positives. The rep might have gone all of the way through delivering a pricing quote and getting a "verbal commitment" from the champion, but if that champion has not engaged and sold to the other buying group members, the purchase will never get done.

Share Rate

One of the challenges that occurs in traditional selling is that when a champion begins sharing information provided by a rep, neither they nor the rep has any way of telling how much the other stakeholders are engaging. Suppose a rep sent a carefully crafted PDF to a champion, who then shares it with their boss. Days afterward, the champion is in the awkward position of having to ask, "Have you looked at it yet?" The rep has no insights into the process either; the rep knows what *they've* done to move the sale forward, but they don't have a clue what is actually going on inside the customer.

Buyer enablement seeks process transparency for both the champion and the rep by tracking the share rate: the percentage of the time that a piece of content gets shared with other stakeholders. For example, if you were to send your prospect an automated video demo, how often does it get shared? If you send 100 video demo links, how many times do they get shared by those viewing them? For example, Table K shows how to review the effectiveness of two different types of content in discovering stakeholders.

TABLE K: SHARE RATE ANALYSIS

Content Type/Title	Number of Invitations to View	Number of Invitations Viewed	Number of Times Shared	Share Rate
Interactive Demo	2440	564	311	55%
Case Study	550	127	12	9%

NOTE: Pay close attention when a prospect shares content; if the number is high, that is an indicator you've found a potential champion.

Buying Stages Each Stakeholder Has Completed

According to Gartner, "Virtually every B2B purchase spans six distinct 'jobs' that buyers must complete to their satisfaction to successfully complete a complex purchase: Problem identification, Solution exploration, Requirements building, Supplier selection, Validation, Consensus creation."[2] Something to consider is tracking your deals along these lines. Which deals have and haven't completed these jobs?

TABLE L: DEAL STATUS

	Problem ID	Solution Exploration	Requirements Building	Supplier Selection	Validation	Reach Consensus
Deal 1	X	X	X			
Deal 2	X					
Deal 3	X	X	X	X	X	
Deal 4	X	X	X	X	X	X
Deal 5	X	X	X			

---

2   Gartner, Win More B2B Sales Deals, Brent Adamson, 2018.

Forecasting Based on Stakeholder Engagement and Alignment

Some data interpretation associated with buyer enablement metrics is straightforward: If a sales rep doesn't have a champion, they need to push to get one. Other analysis requires a little more effort but can be very helpful in determining strategies to sell to any particular buying group. Here are two examples:

Example 1: Identifying Alignment and Misalignment

While all of the analytics are useful, one of the most important analytics must be done manually by the buying coach. It's their responsibility to find, tease out, and then help their champion and other stakeholders work through misalignment in the buying group.

Misalignment may come in many forms. Stakeholders can disagree about anything. But let's go back to the fundamentals of what they need to decide:

- What problem needs solving (the main problem)
- How they should solve it (the main solution)
- What vendor they should use to solve it (the specific vendor)
- When they should solve it (why now?)
- If it's going to be worth the resources required to solve it (ROI)
- If it's going to be worth the effort required to implement and solve it (Emotional ROI)

It makes sense then to analyze how far a group has come in answering these questions in a way that favors your solution. Start by listing the personas in a typical buying group down the side of the chart, including the names of individuals (if known), and list the six questions across the top of the table.

The sales rep should then assign each persona a percentage

ranking: 100% means there is total support for your solution, and 0% means that person is not at all in agreement in that area with you and your champion or that you don't know and need to find out. Negative numbers mean the person is opposed to your solution on that issue.

Table M shows this kind of analysis for a buying group that typically has six personas. In this case, the sales rep can put names to only five of those personas, so the last figure (someone from marketing) is left without a name and has all 0% ratings.

TABLE M: EXAMPLE BUYING GROUP ALIGNMENT ANALYSIS

	Problem	Solution	You as a Vendor	Timeline	$ ROI	Emotional ROI
Oliver (Sales Leader)– Champion	100%	100%	100%	100%	90%	100%
Kristin (End User Manager)	100%	100%	90%	100%	N/A	-30%
Todd (IT InfoSec)	100%	100%	-30%	0%	N/A	50%
Diego (C-Level Exec)	100%	80%	0%	100%	0%	N/A
Jerome (Finance)	75%	50%	50%	50%	-75%	N/A
?? (Marketing Leader)	0%	0%	0%	0%	0%	0%

The first thing this does for you is help you see where the problem spots are or may be. In this example, the sales rep and champion can see that Jerome (in finance), though largely convinced that there is a problem (column 1), does not believe there is a good ROI potential for the proposed solution (column 5). Kristin (end user manager) is mostly on board but *feels* the proposed solution may be the wrong thing to do, and the sale will not go through until she feels an emotional commitment to it. In contrast, Todd (IT) agrees there are problems and likes the proposed solution but does not think the vendor is the right choice.

Once you have determined misalignment, you need to try to understand the misalignment, and then facilitate a conversation between stakeholders who are aligned (especially your champion) and those who aren't.

TIP

Don't try to tackle more than one misaligned stakeholder in the same meeting. In the example, Diego, Jerome, and an undetermined stakeholder are still not aligned on financial ROI. However, Jerome has expressed objections; it's not that he's unaware of the financial ROI you and your champion have proposed. Therefore, he gets a negative number.

It would be unwise to get Jerome in the same conversation as Diego (the C-level exec) until you have Diego's support because Jerome could poison the well.

There is a phenomenon in groups that when one person in the group objects and another is on the fence, the one on the fence almost always takes the side of the objector. The only time you should tackle alignment across multiple misaligned stakeholders at once is at the beginning when you don't know if they have an opinion in these different areas yet or not.

A few instructions and rules of thumb to go by if you decide to do this kind of alignment analysis for a buying group you are working with:

- Your champion may also still need to be educated more before they reach the 100% level on all six factors.
- Given your experience, you may know that some areas don't apply to some stakeholder personas.
- Use +100% to represent a complete vote of confidence; –100% would be a strong blocker in opposition. 0% can mean either

no progress or there is an unknown person (or unfilled persona) on the client's buying group.

* A negative number represents *negative* progress. These are
  your potential blockers.

* If you haven't heard directly from the stakeholder, you can't
  assume 100%, even if another stakeholder tells you they
  are bought in. If your champion tells you they are aligned, I
  recommend putting them at 80%.

Example 2: The Buyer Enablement Way to Forecast Deal Progress and Risk

Every sales professional wants a good forecast of his or her pipeline,
and every sales leader needs an accurate forecast across their team.

Most deal-review discussions go something like this:

Sales Leader: "Tell me about these deals in play."

Account Executive: "Okay, on this deal I've done a need analysis, I've given them a demo, I've addressed their objections and
concerns, I've sent them a proposal, and they said they like it.
I think we're in good shape. Right now, I don't see any major
obstacles, so I give this an 80% likely to close."

And it goes on deal by deal.

The fundamental problem with this approach is that it attempts to
forecast deals based on what the salespeople have done and not what
the buying group looks like, what the champion has done, and what the
buying group at large has accomplished.

Kevin Davis, author of *The Sales Manager's Guide to Greatness*, says:

The data that sales forecasts are based on . . . reflects primarily actions the salespeople have taken, not what the customer has done. So the position that a customer occupies within the funnel—"demo" vs. "trial," for instance—only indicates how far a salesperson has progressed in the steps of selling, not how far a customer has progressed in their decision-making.

. . . While it might sound important to know that a rep has delivered a proposal, simply tracking "proposal delivery" doesn't tell you whether the customer has fully defined their needs or if they understand the economic impact if they do nothing. It doesn't tell you if the customer has compared your offering to those of your competitors, or if they have allocated money for some kind of buying decision. It also can't tell you which (if any) steps the customer has completed in their buying process.[3]

Davis suggests implementing a buying funnel rather than a sales funnel based on the customer actions (exit criteria) that I discussed earlier. At the core of the buying funnel is what he calls the *buy-learning model.* "The label indicates that customers are learning at each step along the way to making a purchase—so selling is really a task of providing customers with the right information at the right time so they can move from one step of buying to another," says Davis.[4]

Davis advocates thinking about the buying process in stages and identifying specific steps that customers typically take at each stage that demonstrate they are progressing through the buying process rather than stalling or leaving the process. He goes so far as to suggest

---

3   Kevin F. Davis, *The Sales Manager's Guide to Greatness: 10 Essential Strategies for Leading Your Team to the Top* (Austin: Greenleaf Book Group, 2017): 91.
4   Davis, *The Sales Manager's Guide to Greatness,* p. 94.

that you should organize your CRM around the buying process rather than the sales process.

I'm a big fan of this approach. By organizing your CRM around what the buyer is doing, you have a much better chance at predicting where on the timeline the deal really is. Moreover, it inherently focuses your sales reps on what the buyer is doing to progress a decision rather than on "what should I be doing next to close this deal?"— which, in my opinion, is ineffective, not to mention bordering on blindly arrogant.

Before changing your CRM, I recommend beginning by changing the way you review deals. As you begin to focus on the progress of the buyer in your deal-review conversations, you will begin to help your reps change their focus and begin to see patterns in buyer behavior across deals that go well and deals that stall.

To implement buyer enablement means that as a sales leader you're going to change the nature of the questions you ask about each deal. They might include questions such as:

- Do you have a champion identified? Tell me how you decided that is the champion.

- What has that champion done so far to promote the deal internally? How is that champion demonstrating that they will take risks to get the purchase complete and the change effected that they want?

- How is the champion responding to your coaching? In what ways have you equipped the champion so far, and how have they used the resources that you've provided?

- How many stakeholders have you discovered? Have you found a stakeholder for each persona in the buying group profile for this product and segment?

- Has each stakeholder engaged, either with you or with the champion? Have they had their questions answered? Do they fit the profile of a typical stakeholder persona, or are they different?

Do you see the difference in the questions? Forecasting using buyer enablement is inherently more accurate because you are asking questions about what the buyers are doing, and they are the only ones who can close the deal.

This new approach doesn't stop with the questions asked of sales reps. The interesting thing about mapping stakeholder alignment is that it creates another data point to help forecast the likelihood to close, not based on what the sales team is doing or has done but rather based on how far along each stakeholder is. There are two ways to do this:

Method 1 (Simple)

One simple way is to average the percentages. Let's look again at the example in Table L, which shows 32 percentages (four of the cells are "not applicable" to that persona so aren't counted), with a numerical sum of 1600%, meaning the average percentage is 1600/32 = 50%. While calculating this percentage is simple, the downside is that it gives all stakeholders equal weight, which usually isn't true. That said, it is simple, and looking at this deal from the outside, my gut says that 50% likelihood to close might not be too far off.

Method 2 (Weighted Negative)

Not all stakeholders carry the same weight when it comes to decision-making, and often those opposed to change can stall progress more easily than those who support a change can move it forward. To accommodate this fact, another method for estimating the likelihood that a deal will close is to give more weight to some stakeholders than others and adjust the numbers to account for people who are opposed to the purchase of your solution.

In this method, you would weight each stakeholder on a scale of 1 (least influential) to 5 (most influential), then multiply any negative percentage by that weight. Also add an additional negative 10% in each category to a stakeholder persona that hasn't been identified yet.

Table N shows the results when these adjustments are applied to the same data in Table M. When you take into account the influence of the various buyers in this group, the average likelihood to close has dropped down to 38%—probably more realistic given that in this deal there are three potential blockers and a stakeholder who hasn't been identified yet.

TABLE N: WEIGHTED NEGATIVE BUYING GROUP ALIGNMENT

	Weight	Problem	Solution	You as a Vendor	Timeline	$ ROI	Emotional ROI
Oliver (Sales Leader)– Champion	3	100%	100%	100%	100%	90%	100%
Kristin (End User Manager)	2	100%	100%	90%	100%	N/A	-60%
Todd (IT InfoSec)	5	100%	100%	-150%	0%	N/A	50%
Diego (C-Level Exec)	5	100%	80%	0%	100%	0%	N/A
Jerome (Finance)	4	75%	50%	50%	50%	-240%	N/A
(Marketing Leader)	3	-10%	-10%	-10%	-10%	-10%	-10%

TECHNOLOGY TIP

When looking for technology to help you, try to find technology that will show stakeholder alignment for the category that software is helping you with. For example, if you are using a financial ROI tool to deliver ROI calculations to the stakeholders, does it help you see how stakeholders are engaging with the ROI and how they react or adjust the ROI calculations? This might help you see misalignment faster.

As another example, in the Consensus intelligent demo automation software, you can see quickly on the Buyer Matrix view where there is alignment or misalignment across stakeholders based on what is driving their particular interests.

More Information = Better Strategies

I find the kinds of metrics covered in this chapter to be one of the most exciting aspects of buyer enablement. Instead of looking at deal quality by what the salespeople are doing, we are looking at deal quality by the actual personas and people that have to get involved to get the deal done. Using this approach, you have a clearer picture of how likely you are to get a deal done and what work needs to be done to get there.

Remember that you'll need to do some CRM setup before this becomes practical. In early pilot stages I recommend running some of these kinds of analyses with just a few reps and deals via a simple spreadsheet. If you and your reps believe this will be a valuable approach, you can go to the effort to systematize it in the CRM for the whole team.

CHAPTER 14

UNDERSTANDING DEMO AUTOMATION

"Through machinery, man can exert tremendous powers almost as
fantastic as if he were the hero of a fairy tale."
—MARIA MONTESSORI

There are at least four different types of information that buying
groups need before they will sign on the dotted line. They need to:

- Learn enough about your product or solution to decide that it
  has excellent potential for solving their problem or enabling
  them to capture the opportunity they are looking for
- Have their questions and concerns answered
- Analyze and believe that the investment will financially and
  emotionally pay off
- Have enough evidence of success from other customers to
  believe the associated risks are worth taking (social proof)

Unless you succeed at the first of these, the others don't matter.
Because I've spent the last five years working on technology solutions
to help teams succeed at this, I am dedicating two chapters to what I
consider to currently be one of the most inefficient processes in B2B

sales today: the product demo. Let's address the concerns about live vs. automated demos, discuss different types of demos, and explore which can be automated to speed up the buying process.

Pros and Cons of Live Demos

Doing live demos has its benefits. During a live demo you often:

- **Get a good read on the customer's interest in certain aspects of your product.** You might hear things like, "Wow, I really like that feature" or "That is critical to us" or "We don't need that capability."

- **Discover how to personalize your messages.** Through interaction with the attendees, you can find out what is truly most important to the customer and what is not (e.g., you can pick up on whether the customer's reaction to a topic is "Can you move on—we've seen enough of this section?" or "Can we look deeper into this part of your solution?").

- **Discover and potentially engage other members of the buying group** (e.g., "Wow, this has been a great demo. Can we set up another time to show it to some other people in our organization?").

Because of these benefits, most sales organizations consider the live demo—either face-to-face or remotely via web conferencing—to be a pivotal moment in the sales process. You learn the needs of key stakeholders, gather them together, and demonstrate your capability to deliver the results they want. They ask a few questions and you win the deal, right? Unfortunately, that's not how it usually goes. Here's a more common scenario:

1. The initial prospect wants a demo early in the sales process, so you or your sales engineer gives a splash demo—a short

summary demo to help the prospect get some understanding without releasing too much information too early.

2. The enthusiastic prospect starts telling their colleagues and leaders about what they saw. They butcher the message, not understanding what is most important to each stakeholder. They get resistance. They tell the stakeholders, "Well, you just have to see it. Let me line up a demo with the sales rep for you so you can see it yourself."

3. You line up another demo for other stakeholders. You ask them questions about what is driving their interest in this solution, and (if you're good) you tailor the demo to their unique needs. They get quite interested and begin to discuss internally with other stakeholders.

4. Repeat steps one through three at least five to six times.

I've spoken with salespeople and sales engineers who end up giving some kind of demo more than ten times before they can close the deal. Scheduling demo after demo often adds weeks or months to the sales cycle as you accommodate calendars. The seemingly continual churn drives down close rates and extends sales cycles.

Add to this the common problem of running into technical bugs, or even crashes, during the live demonstration, and it can be a frustrating experience for everyone. To try to prevent this, one senior sales enablement leader I spoke to at one of the world's largest software companies said they have an entire team of 20 developers who build and maintain the live demo system.

Ask any B2B sales professional if their demos are an efficient part of selling, and they'll almost always respond with a resounding *no*. But though they'll tell you how time-consuming and repetitive demos can be, they will also say that the demo is one, if not the most, important and essential step in the sales process. Why so cold and hot? Because their experience shows that demos are critical to buyers making a decision (even though oftentimes the demo participants aren't buyers at all: they are just checking it out for some future day, months or even years from now).

The ultimate problem, according to Peter Cohan, author of *Great Demo!* (a gold-standard guide to giving effective software demos), is that when he surveyed hundreds of his readers, they said that at least 50% of their demos were considered "wasted," meaning it seemed like a good idea at the time, but in hindsight it was time spent with poorly qualified prospects, or the time spent in the demo was on things the prospect really didn't care about. Peter goes on to say:

So we do more and more and more demos to try to fill the pipeline. And the faster we go, the behinder we get (to paraphrase Lewis Carroll). Our true productivity is frankly pretty poor . . .[1]

In a recent survey of over 460 sales engineers, more than half of the participants reported that at least 30% of their demos were unqualified.[2]

Scaling Sales Engineers (Presales) Is Almost Impossible

Another key problem with live demos is that they impose enormous scaling pressure on operations.

The demo function in SaaS companies is often performed by sales engineers, often called solution consultants, because of their ability to understand the problem the buying group wants to solve and customize a live demonstration to help them see the vendor can solve the problem for them.

This group of technical professionals is also called "presales"

1 Peter Cohan, "Rescue—From the Tyranny of Traditional Demos," LinkedIn, September 26, 2018, https://www.linkedin.com/pulse/rescue-from-tyranny-traditional-demos-peter-cohan/.
2 2020 Sales Engineer Compensation and Workload Report, Consensus Sales, https://www.goconsensus.com/resources

because it is considered a critical step before the sale can take place. The sales team asks for more and more demos as their team grows or as marketing demand increases. Presales teams often struggle to keep up with the increasing demand for live demos. This function is often understaffed and overworked, creating a huge bottleneck, derailing opportunities, and frustrating sales teams and customers with unavoidable delays.

In fact, I've been asking dozens of sales and presales leaders this question: "How long does it take to train a sales rep vs. a sales engineer?"

The response for sales reps? Four to six months.

The response for sales engineers? Two to three years.

This creates a natural problem when it comes to scaling the sales team. You want to hire 100 new sales reps, but you'll need a corresponding 25–35 sales engineers to support those hires. There is no way to scale the presales team effectively when it takes four to six times longer to train a presales rep compared to a sales rep.

Moving Down-Market Presents Another Presales Scaling Conundrum

Many SaaS companies are trying to uncover new growth opportunities or prevent competitive disruption by selling to smaller companies than they are used to. This is often called selling down-market.

Moving down-market presents a similar scaling challenge. Smaller target companies usually equal smaller deal sizes. Suppose that to hit an $850,000 quota selling up-market requires closing 3.4 deals when the average deal size is $250,000. If your close rate is 25%, you need to be working 14 opportunities to reach the target.

Now suppose that you are tasked with going down-market with a team that closes deals averaging $70,000. To reach the same $850,000 target, you would have to close 12.2 deals and work 49 opportunities.

The same presales process of high-touch live demos is never going to work when selling down-market.

JOB THREAT OR JOB SECURITY FOR
SOLUTION CONSULTANTS?

Solution consultants and sales engineers are in high demand. As of the writing of this book, LinkedIn showed more than 20,000 open positions, just in the United States. Most people I know in those positions are overworked and finding it hard to keep up with all of the requests for demos. Yet still there's a concern that demo automation could eliminate some of these jobs.

That has not been the case in my experience. Instead, interactive demos eliminate the most repetitive parts of the solution consultant's job, but it will never replace them entirely. Interactive demo automation will free up dozens, maybe hundreds, of hours each year so that the consultants and engineers can spend their time with buyers having strategic conversations and preparing and delivering the highly technical demos and solution recommendations that they are uniquely suited to provide.

With demo automation, these professionals are able to handle more demo requests in less time. When a sales rep asks for a standard demo for a product, the consultant simply provides them with a trackable link to the demo, and they have spent two minutes on this task rather than an hour prepping for and delivering the demo.

Demo automation is your Iron Man suit that makes you more capable, not something that will replace you (Figure 33).

SOLUTION CONSULTANT

SOLUTION CONSULTANT
WITH DEMO AUTOMATION

Figure 33.

The Case for Interactive Demo Automation

If you're a sales engineer, fitting the standard demo into your work life can be challenging. You know you can't get rid of it, but having to do so many of them for underqualified prospects just seems too difficult to manage.

Because demos (even standard demos) are absolutely crucial in the decision-making process, we can't just abandon them altogether. But as I've just discussed, doing live product demos (whether in person or using web-based screen sharing) comes with heavy baggage that makes a compelling argument for at least some automation:

- **It's time-consuming and expensive.**

    Often, a demo takes 45–60 minutes (and sometimes much more than that). Add to that the fact the salesperson has to provide the demo multiple times, as I just discussed. Plus, if it's an in-person demo, it most likely requires travel expenses, which can add up fast. Calculating the labor costs alone can terrify even the bravest business leaders.

- **It draws out the sales cycle.**

  It can often take two to three weeks to coordinate schedules for each demo. If the sales rep has to do this multiple times to reach all the stakeholders, we're talking between three to five months before the rep can close the sale. It's no wonder some companies have yearlong sales cycles!

- **It requires a high level of expertise.**

  Many organizations employ demo specialists who spend years learning their product lines. Often known as sales engineers or solution consultants, these people are in high demand. And because it takes a long time to train people to get to the required level of expertise, they are a scarce resource.

- **It's not scalable . . . at all.**

  Because they're live and take up so much time, live demos put an incredible amount of drag on your organization's ability to scale. Each sales professional has a limited caseload they can handle. Moreover, each new salesperson or sales engineer has to learn how to do the demo, taking longer to ramp up new team members.

- **It's not repeatable or predictable.**

  Every salesperson or sales engineer does the demo differently. This adds a huge amount of variability to your messaging and customer experience and makes quality control a pipe dream.

- **It forces you to pick and choose which prospects get the best service.**

  Because you cannot do a live demo for everyone, you have to choose which potential customers get live demos and which don't, potentially leaving large segments of potential customers grossly underserved.

- **There are huge opportunity costs.**

  Have you ever asked yourself the question, "What would my sales people be doing if they could reduce the amount of time they spend doing product demos by 75%?" Hopefully the answer to this question isn't "improving their golf swing." Strategic consulting and architecting solutions for key prospects and customers comes to mind.

Both increased hiring in the sales team and the need some companies have to move down-market make the case for demo automation. If you are involved in either of these initiatives, I highly recommend you look into interactive demo automation.

Again, I'm not suggesting you completely replace your live demos but instead reduce how many you do and make the ones you do wildly more efficient and effective. Bring multiple stakeholders to your demo educated and ready to talk specifics. Understand ahead of time what is driving each stakeholder's unique interests and where there is alignment and misalignment across the buying group.

Four Types of Demos

After observing sales processes, and particularly demo processes, in dozens of B2B sales organizations, it's clear to me that some kinds of live demos are more easily replaced by automated versions than others. To explain what I mean, consider four different types, roughly correlating with stages in the buying process:

1. Vision demo
2. Qualifying demo
3. Technical demo
4. Closing demo

Vision Demos

The conflict about when to provide a demo usually arises because when vendors (and analysts apparently) think of a demo, they envision a 45-minute (at least) deep dive that is delivered by the sales engineer. Buyers don't need or want that kind of depth and detail up front. They'll need it eventually, but not at the beginning.

What they want early is what Peter Cohan, author of *Great Demo!*, calls the *vision demo*. This type of demo effectively outlines the problem you solve, the benefit of solving the problem, how you've solved it for similar customers, and a quick look at the product itself without going into too many details. This gets the client what they want and still accomplishes the main objective of the first meeting: to establish a strong value proposition. The emphasis during the vision demo is on the problem, solution, and benefit—in short, the value, not on detailed features.

Vision demos are great candidates for automation because they can be short and very visual. Still, if you want to do them live, Peter Cohan has some useful tips.

PETER COHAN'S TIPS FOR DOING A LIVE VISION DEMO

If you're going to do it live (rather than a self-directed interactive demo), Peter recommends this sequence for the vision demo:

1. Start with a menu of topics that they can choose from and ask them what is most important to them to cover.
2. Lead out with an informal success story that begins with "Here's how we helped similar heads of sales at . . ."
3. Then ask the question: "How does this compare with your situation?" This leads them into a self-analysis and discovery conversation where they are talking about their own problems.
4. Follow up with "You've asked for a demo. Would you like an example of how another customer has solved the same problem that you're addressing?"

5. After completing the second customer story, share a "demo" that is just screenshots of key parts of the application that you know they are interested in and talk about the main benefit that part of the application provides.
6. End with "Is this the kind of thing that you have in mind?"
7. Then finally, "If you're willing to answer some questions, we can put together a deeper tailored demo . . ."

Qualifying Demos

How many demos do your sales engineers do for underqualified leads? A qualifying demo helps you further qualify the prospect before you engage sales engineers. A qualifying demo is still a standard demo, but it goes deeper into features and functionality than the vision demo. Live, this demo usually takes 40 to 60 minutes. A qualifying demo is usually going to range from 10 to 20 minutes in length when automated.

Remember, at every stage the demo should reinforce the benefits and main value proposition that is important to the buying group. So even though you are diving deeper into features, you have to continually reinforce why that feature is important to the value proposition.

Use Interactive Video Demos to Qualify Presales Resources

"Gartner research shows that the majority of technology buyers (59%) that regularly make purchases will 'always' or 'often' respond to vendor marketing campaigns when they are not in an active buying process."[3]

Further, "doing hundreds of one-on-one demos is not an effective

---

3   Gartner "Tech Go-to-Market: Best Practices for Emerging Technology Providers to Identify 'Real' Leads," Michele Buckley, September 18, 2018.

use of sales resources and, in time, may reveal a low conversion rate and create frustration all around." Qualifying prospects before engaging sales-engineering staff for live demos has become perhaps the biggest scaling challenge across the software industry. A recent study among presales professionals shows that half of respondents said that 30% of their demos were not effectively qualified. (See Figure 34.[4]) That's a huge inefficiency.

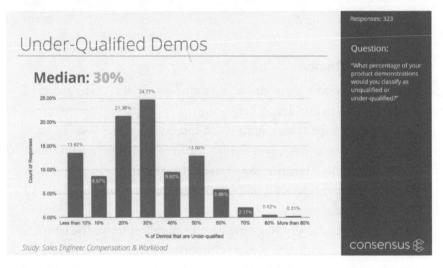

Figure 34.

Additional research from Gartner also highlights this challenge:

A call to action that mentions a demo likely will get interest, as 58% of buyers cited 'demonstrations' as a call to action they would respond to in a marketing campaign. Similarly, 50% of buyers surveyed cite demonstrations as one of the most valuable supplied marketing materials during the buying cycle for new IT providers' purchases.

4   Consensus, "2020 Sales Engineer Salary Compensation and Workload," January 16, 2020, https://www.goconsensus.com/sales/presales/webinar-sales-engineer-salary-workload/.

High volumes of one-on-one demos waste time and cost of sales in an emerging technology provider, particularly one with new and innovative technology. As shown in the previous figures, it's highly likely that buyers who are not in an active purchase process will accept offers for demos, resulting in a growing volume of demonstrations without any increase in revenue." [5]

Example: Using an Interactive Automated Demo to Qualify "Real" Deals

Some presales teams are beginning to use interactive demo automation to help qualify more effectively. One sales leader running an inside sales team for Oracle was struggling to get support from the solution-consulting team because it was overloaded with leads. He was encountering the many problems with demos I've discussed, such as having to wait several days before a demo could be scheduled for the prospect (using up sales cycle time) and having people attend who weren't really interested in buying yet.

This problem was not unique to the presales team at Oracle. Remember the statistic from Peter Cohan, who discovered that 50% of his survey respondents thought demos were "wasted"? The presales team at Oracle built a library of reusable interactive qualifying demos that the sales team could use to send out to a prospect immediately when the prospect wanted the demo. If the prospect watched it and shared it with others in their organization, then Oracle considered those actions a qualifier to allocate a presales resource for a deeper dive with that prospect. This has worked so well that they've moved toward proactively sending the demo to prospects as a qualifying gauge.

"Now when we get a prospect that says she is serious and wants to schedule a meeting with us, we send her a Consensus automated demo. Let's see how real she is," said the sales leader. "Let's say that we

5   Gartner "Tech Go-to-Market: Best Practices for Emerging Technology Providers to Identify 'Real' Leads," Michele Buckley, September 18, 2018.

see she didn't even open it. How real is that meeting going to be if she won't even open it or share it?"

Using engagement with interactive demos early in the sales process to gauge qualification can reduce the burden on your presales team all while helping prospects get the information they need. This frees up presales resources to be more responsive to those deals that are truly qualified.

Demo Qualified Lead (DQL): The Missing Lead-Qualification Stage

Most sales organizations use a series of named lead stages to categorize leads into groups of more and more qualification. While the specifics may vary by organization, most organizations will use some or more of the following:

- Inquiry (INQ): a contact who has not shown any purchasing behavior but wants to follow your company

- Marketing Qualified Lead (MQL): a contact who has "raised their hand" and expressed interest in learning more about a specific product or solution

- Sales Accepted Lead (SAL): a lead who has been nurtured by marketing enough to engage with sales

- Sales Qualified Lead (SQL): a lead who has shown some intent to purchase

- Qualified Opportunity: a prospect and buying group that demonstrate strong intent to purchase within a specific time frame and with budget

Where in this typical lead-qualification process are we qualifying the lead before engaging presales resources? The very fact that the industry has no official stage for this suggests that it undervalues the impact sales engineers have on pipeline acceleration. It is an overlooked step ripe for optimization. That's why we've come up with a new stage designation: the Demo Qualified Lead (DQL). What is a DQL? It's a lead or prospect who has been through enough qualification gates to merit the allocation of live sales-engineering resources. In other words, they are qualified enough to get a live demo from a presales professional.

As you try to decide how to better qualify leads for sales-engineering resources, consider formally implementing the DQL stage in your lead-qualification process. I recommend that the presales and sales teams at your organization get together and determine what defines a DQL. This effort alone will help reduce the number of unqualified demos being delivered by your presales team. Also consider using interactive demo automation as a part of your DQL qualification process. If they won't engage with an automated demo that takes a few minutes, do you really want to spend some of your company's most valuable and costly resources (the sales engineers) on that prospect?

Technical Demos

The technical demo is the one type of demo that may not be a good candidate for demo automation. It usually involves a deep dive into product use (installation, operation, support, etc.) tailored specifically at the problem the buying group is trying to solve at their company. Most enterprise software vendors tailor this demo to the specific situation of the customer, even loading the demo version with data from the customer as a Proof of Concept. Live technical demos can range from a couple of hours to several days, depending on the complexity of the problem and proposed solution.

Even if you do choose not to automate the technical demo, keep in mind that an automated standard demo can act as an important follow-up that the buying group can give to other secondary stakeholders who weren't able to make it to the technical demo. Quite often, secondary stakeholders don't want or need to see the full technical demo.

Also, if the deal is worth spending days or weeks getting the technical demo ready, it may also be a good idea to create a unique automated version of the technical demo as a follow-up instead of a standard automated demo.

Closing Demos

Once a buying group has narrowed their final selection to a few vendors, they begin thinking about how they will implement the solution, and their questions turn from main benefit and functionality to a lot of secondary, but necessary, elements required for them to make a final decision. These could include things like:

- How your system integrates with other platforms
- How you comply with data protection standards, such as GDPR
- What the onboarding and implementation processes look like

In many cases, a simple automated demo of each particular area will be sufficient for them to move forward without engaging you in further conversations. Closing demos are shorter, more targeted demos aimed at answering specific questions about implementation.

Summary of Demo Types

Table O summarizes the features and uses of the four types of demos. As you can see, technical demos in particular need to be so detailed in nature and so customized to the client that they would be hard to automate, or it would be undesirable to miss out on the engaging back-and-forth that comes during that demo experience.

TABLE O: SUMMARY OF DEMO TYPES

	Description	General Buying Journey Stage	Good for Automation?
Vision Demo	5-10 minutes. Answers two questions: "How will my life be better if I choose this solution?" and "Can you show me a quick look at how your solution works?"	Very early Sometimes used by Product Marketing or BDRs	Yes
Qualifying Demo	15-20 minutes. Answers this need: "I saw the solution initially and was interested. Now I want to get a good understanding of how it works in general and how the usability is." It also answers the question for the sales team: "Is this a real deal or are they just kicking the tires?" If they are the real deal, the sales team often begins to ask for more support from presales.	Early In forward-thinking organizations, often performed by inside sales reps or a special qualifying team; sometimes performed by sales engineers	Yes
Technical Demo	45 minutes to several hours. Driven by deep discovery from the presales and sales team, the technical demo (or demos) satisfies the needs of clients' technical requirements; often highly customized.	Mid to late Usually delivered by sales engineers on the presales team	Sometimes, though you should consider using an automated demo as a pass-along to other secondary stakeholders who couldn't make it
Closing Demo	5-10 minutes each. Closing demos answer questions about satellite needs such as product add-ons, customer support, professional services, other future integrations, etc.	Late	Yes

That said, three out of the four demo categories can clearly benefit from automation. In the rest of this chapter, whenever I talk about automating demos, remember that I'm specifically referring to vision, qualifying, and closing demos.

Automating a Standard Demo with Interactive Demo Automation

Perhaps the most fertile opportunity for leveraging interactive demo automation is with a standard demo. This is sometimes called the "vanilla demo" or the "splash demo." Quite often, very expensive sales engineers' time is used up doing repetitive demos for early stage prospects engaging in the sales process.

Sales engineers who do a lot of standard demos often say they are tired of being "the demo monkey" or "the demo parrot" because they are repeating themselves over and over. During my interviews with sales leaders, some companies reported that as much as 60% of the sales engineers' time is used doing standard demos. One important negative side effect of this is that the sales-engineering team morale declines as they spend more and more of their time doing brainless repetitive demos.

If you could automate this part of the process, your sales engineers could be spending more of their time having strategic conversations. Not only will this drive better financial results for your company, but also morale will grow and employee retention will increase because the sales engineers are spending more of their time on activities that use their intelligence.

Providing Demos Throughout the Buyer Journey

On the one hand, many buyers want a demo more than anything else. On the other, vendors are counseled to avoid demonstrating too early. So how do you get the buyer what they want and still keep them out of the quagmire that can develop by giving them too much information up front? Try following one of these approaches:

- Place a "Request a Demo" button on your website or as a call to action in your early outreach.

- Provide buyers with an abbreviated live demo, but limit it to screenshots placed inside a slide deck rather than demonstrating from the live system. The objective of the demo at this stage is to articulate the overall value of your solution and not drown them in features.

- Use the solution I've been advocating in this book: Provide buyers with a self-directed interactive demo that they can access at will and share with anyone else inside their organization. Interactive demos allow the buyers to customize the demo to their unique interests so they get a look at some aspects of the product whenever they want. (My company, Consensus, was specifically founded to provide a place where software sellers can get help building interactive demos.) Remember, when building interactive demos for consumption early in the buying process, keep them focused on the main benefits of each part of your solution rather than too deep on feature functionality.

Whether you offer live demos or interactive demos (or a mix of both) to your prospects, make sure they are effective. Ineffectively prepared or delivered demos can actually cause more problems. If prospects don't understand what they're seeing, fail to see the relevance of what you're demonstrating to their situation, or fail to address objections that you can anticipate, you'll end up with a longer buying cycle, or worse yet, they'll abandon you as a potential solution. On the other hand, if your demo is an excellent tailored demonstration, delivered well, and connects the dots to their requirements, then it will actually help shorten the sales cycle and you'll have a greater chance of success.

ACTION TIP

Keep in mind, however, that "effective" doesn't necessarily mean polished, time-consuming, or high production value. Interestingly, there is strong evidence that less-polished content comes across as more genuine and helpful.

Still Skeptical About Automation?

I sometimes hear: "The demo is such an important step where I connect with the customer and get a read on them that I just can't afford to automate it." Many sales and presales professionals struggle to believe that something as interpersonal and engaging as a live demo can be or should be automated.

While I empathize with their concerns, these are many of the same concerns that came up in the e-learning industry when corporate training teams began to adopt self-directed online learning as a solution. "How can we replace a live trainer in the classroom?" was the cry. In spite of the concerns and because of the huge benefits of scale, self-directed e-learning courses have taken a rightful place in the technology stack of almost every size of organization. Content experts and trainers have become course-building gurus. Yes, some courses are still best taught in person. But e-learning courses have freed up those key trainers to spend their time and focus on topics that require critical live training where e-learning isn't a good fit.

The same will be true for demo automation. As I discussed earlier, not all types of demos are suited for automation. Thus, automation won't replace all live demos, but it should replace a good many demos. If you don't automate some of your demo process, your competitors will and gain strong advantages over you with their added efficiencies—maintaining presales margins that scale with growing sales teams and coverage in different language markets.

Similarly, what exactly is meant by "automation" matters. If you try to automate demos by just posting a WebEx recording or YouTube video, then yes, you will miss out on gaining the kinds of information I talked about in this chapter. And you really aren't automating the demo by just posting some videos because demo automation technology should largely mimic what you would do in a live demo: ask questions and tailor the demo to their unique interests.

Don't get me wrong; automation isn't going to replace personal interaction. It will simply make those interactions exponentially more efficient and effective.

Remember, buyer enablement is about delivering what your champion needs when they need it. Since getting a demo is the number one type of content prospects want, delivering it when they want it rather than having to wait on sales or presales resources is critical to helping the buying process be as efficient as possible.

CHAPTER 15

HOW DOES AN INTERACTIVE DEMO ACTUALLY WORK?

"Automation is to your time what compounding interest is to your money."

—RORY VADEN[1]

Now that I've discussed the requirements, needs, and uses for interactive demos, it's time to pull everything together to see how it works in practice.

The Consensus Software in Action

An interactive automated demo constructs a customized video timeline on the fly for each viewer depending upon their interests and priorities. But before that can happen, you need to define your content and build the reusable asset that will be sent to the different stakeholders in the buying group.

---

1 Rory Vaden, *Procrastinate on Purpose: 5 Permissions to Multiply Your Time* (New York: TarcherPerigee, 2015): 98.

Step 1: Build the content pieces, build the demo

Basically, your team has to define the topics for a particular demo and then develop and upload video clips and documents related to those topics. Through Consensus, buyers' choices about what interests them will determine whether they see a longer clip or a shorter clip. So you'll need to have both long and short clips linked to each topic.

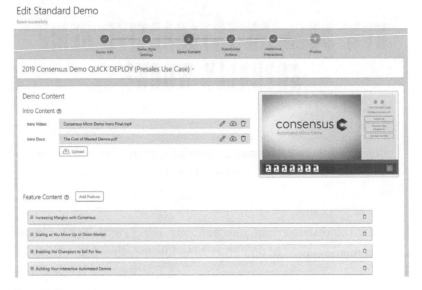

Figure 35: Content pieces.

Step 2: Share a link to a custom portal with champion and/or other stakeholders

Figure 36: Custom portal entry point.

Step 3: Identify the person's role

The potential buyer answers a question about their role:

Figure 37: Identify the role.

Step 4: Discover their interests

When the viewer selects a role, the demo branches to a personalized sub-demo targeted at that role and asks them additional questions about what is most important to them personally (Figure 38):

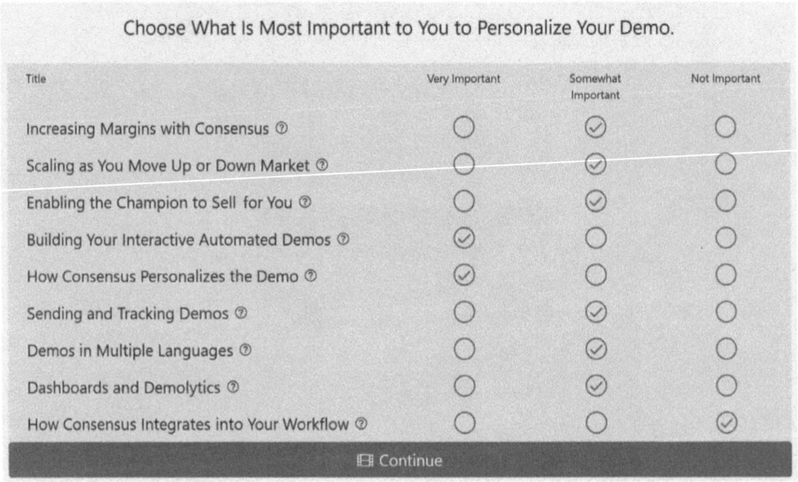

Choose What Is Most Important to You to Personalize Your Demo.

Title	Very Important	Somewhat Important	Not Important
Increasing Margins with Consensus ⑦	○	⊘	○
Scaling as You Move Up or Down Market ⑦	○	⊘	○
Enabling the Champion to Sell for You ⑦	○	⊘	○
Building Your Interactive Automated Demos ⑦	⊘	○	○
How Consensus Personalizes the Demo ⑦	⊘	○	○
Sending and Tracking Demos ⑦	○	⊘	○
Demos in Multiple Languages ⑦	○	⊘	○
Dashboards and Demolytics ⑦	○	⊘	○
How Consensus Integrates into Your Workflow ⑦	○	○	⊘

▤ Continue

Figure 38: Identifying interests.

Step 5: The software generates a personalized demo

The demo automation platform then curates all of the available video clips, documents them related to the stakeholder's choices, and then stitches together the relevant video clips based on the viewer's interests. The demo leads with those things they marked very important, follows with what they marked somewhat important, and skips the things they marked not important. Note: For very important features, a longer clip is shown than for somewhat important features. Unimportant features are not shown at all (Figure 39). This way, each person receives a complete demo tailored in content and length.

Figure 39: Clip length varies.

As you can see, once you have the various forms of content prepared, the process of using interactive demos is quick and painless—and generates data you and your champion will find useful. If you want to experience a self-directed automated demo, visit buyerenablement.io.

Interactive Demo Case Studies

Can something so easy for the buyer to use really have an impact? Here are two stories from Consensus clients that prove it's possible.

CASE STUDY #1: An Enterprise Software Company Scales Presales While Going Down-Market by Enabling Buyers with Adaptive Video Demos

One of the world's largest software companies—used to selling into other large enterprises at low volume and very large deal sizes—was getting disrupted from the bottom by emerging competition. They were also looking for a new market in which they could grow their top-line revenue.

Up to this point, the company had largely ignored smaller mid-market companies, since those were considered outside their target demographic. With a new initiative, they began marketing and selling into smaller companies through what they called their commercial sales team.

Their typical model was to use solution consultants to analyze the customer's goals and then provide and demo a recommended solution. They quickly discovered this model was not scalable at the higher volumes needed to close at the lower end of the market. Their margins suffered, and their solution-consulting team could not keep up with the rapidly increasing demands for demos coming from the sales team. Costs grew in lockstep with volume.

Exacerbating the problem was the need to deliver demos in nine different language markets. The company would typically send a sales rep, a solution consultant, and a translator to deliver the demos in person, sometimes making multiple trips.

Tod, a senior director of sales consulting, and Oliver, his executive VP, were tasked with coming up with a solution to protect margins while still hitting sales targets at high volume.

Tod described the challenge: "The cost of doing business needed to go down, and we needed to strip a considerable amount of money from our operating costs."

Despite an effort to use an in-house video-hosting platform, Tod and Oliver felt strongly that prospects needed a platform that would map content to their individual stakeholder interests and concerns the way a live demo can. That way, each buyer could get the information they needed immediately and share it with other stakeholders without having to wait for (scarce) solution-consulting resources to be made available.

They selected a specific team of 30 presales reps and the 125 inside sales reps whom those presales reps worked with to implement their buyer enablement solution. Here's a summary of this company's story:

- **PROFILE:** Large enterprise SaaS company with deal sizes in the millions needed to figure out how to make a profitable sales process when going down-market (deals less than $100,000).

- **GOAL:** Scale the presales product demonstration function down-market by enabling buyers with interactive video demos instead of live demos.

- **IMPLEMENTATION:** The sales team began equipping their internal champions with automated video demos that they could share with other stakeholders. These video demos were based on Consensus technology that would automatically adapt to each stakeholder's unique interests in response to stakeholders' answers to key questions.

- **IMPACT:** The results are shown in Figure 40.

Results

3,200	Total number of automated micro-demos sent.
12,800	Total presales man hours saved through the use of automated micro-demos; equivalent to 6.2 FTEs.
$738,462	Value of time savings based solely upon presales rep salary. This does not account for benefits accrued from faster response times, consistent messaging, or travel savings, etc.
$75K	Highest individual deal value closed exclusively through demo automation, i.e. *without any face to face engagement*.
$4K	Average cost of an international onsite, which have been largely eliminated through demo automation.

Figure 40: Results in Case #1.

- The sales team was able to immediately deliver the product education the buyers needed, as well as content that kept the message consistent yet tailored to each stakeholder.

- The sales team still required help from the solution-consulting team but reduced those requests by 57%.

- The sales team began closing deals as high as $75,000 with no solution-consulting resources required (i.e., they used only automated demos).

- The presales team was able to avoid hiring 13 additional presales reps, which enabled them to maintain their margins while servicing growing demands for product demos.

- **CONCLUSION**: Being provided the better information and analytics, the champions in the buying groups were able to better meet the needs of different stakeholders using prebuilt resources rather than having to rely on appointment after appointment involving sales reps to get the deal done.

DID YOU CATCH HOW BUYER ENABLEMENT EASED TALENT REQUIREMENTS?

The company from case number one and other Consensus clients have discovered that pouring their expertise into developing relevant, targeted, segmented video clips that can be compiled into custom videos has made it easier for sales reps with moderate skills to sell more effectively.

According to Gartner, "Sales organizations that design their buyer enablement approaches well rely less on the ability of individual reps to provide buyers with helpful information. Targeted information for individual buyers requires less in-the-moment critical thinking, which lessens the burden to hire for or train specific rep capabilities."

Further, sales reps can be described as an "information authority" or an "information connector." Gartner defines information connectors as follows: "These reps serve as curators or brokers of information rather than individual experts. They largely focus on finding and directing customers to the right information, tools and data rather than relying on individual experience."

Gartner research shows that "the 'information connector' increases the likelihood of purchase ease by 40%, while the 'information authority' increases it by just 10%."[2]

---

2   Gartner, *Win More B2B Sales Deals*, Brent Adamson, 2018.

CASE STUDY #2: A Midmarket SaaS Company Tests ROI on Automated Demos

One midmarket medical software company based in the United States adopted Consensus's demo automation platform as part of a buyer enablement strategy. This company sells into doctors' offices and health-care systems where the buying group typically includes office managers, nurses, and of course, medical physicians. One of the bigger challenges they had is that to get a deal done, all doctors had to approve, so there was no final decision maker. They needed unanimity.

Getting the doctors' attention was one hurdle, and then getting them all to agree was another. In the meantime, they needed to persuade the entire buying group that the pain of switching out their current medical software system was worth it.

Jessica, a sales operations leader, was tasked with overseeing the implementation and justification for the software and change in strategy. She wanted to measure ROI, so she set up a specific test for the first 90 days from launch using an A/B split test. She assigned 80 sales reps to the project and asked them to send the self-directed adaptive video demos from the Consensus platform on every other deal. The other half of deals they would run the same way they always had—manually discovering and engaging each stakeholder.

Given that each rep would typically run about 40 deals a quarter at a 32% close rate, across 80 reps, the split test would compare results from about 3,200 deals in progress, roughly 1,600 deals in each group.

Here is a summary of this company's story:

- **PROFILE**: Midmarket SaaS company with $12,000 average deal size and a 65-day sales cycle.

- **GOAL**: The company was looking to accelerate the sales process even though multiple stakeholders, such as office managers, nurses, and doctors, often needed to buy in on the solution despite rarely being in the same room.

- **KEY POINTS**: The company believed that an automated video demo with a focused message around what's important for each stakeholder would:

- Shorten the sales cycle or decrease time to close
- Ensure correct messaging gets to the right people
- Reduce the number of additional live demos needed to
- same prospect
- Allow sales rep and sales engineer to do more live demos to key prospects and accounts
- Show what is important to every stakeholder or decision maker by showing analytics on what they view

• **RESULTS:** After 90 days they compared the deals that used pre-built automated demos to enable the buying group with those that they did the old way. Compared to the status quo deals, the deals where the reps enabled their buyers with adaptive video demos designed to engage and personalize to each stakeholder showed a 44% increase in the close rate and remarkably a 62% reduction in the sales cycle (Figure 41).

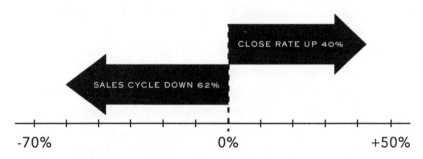

-70%   0%   +50%

Figure 41: Case Study Results: For the medical software company in the featured case study, use of Consensus technology and buyer enablement strategies generated a 62% reduction in the length of the sales cycle and a 44% increase in close rates.

One account executive named Brian said, "I sent the video demo to the billing manager, who sent it to the doctor, who watched it, who sent it to two others in the office. The doctor loved what he saw. We did a brief demo today, which sealed the deal."

- **CONCLUSION:** While Jessica and her team focused solely on the stakeholder education piece using demo automation, even this one step forward in enabling their buyers gave them massive results. Four years later, this company has expanded its buyer enablement approach and library of video demo content and is still seeing similar results.

Lower Your Expectations: Less-Professional Production = Greater Engagement

What's the first leading indicator that you have a strong product demo video? Engagement. That's how long viewers spend watching your video (or maybe rewatching it). So the better the video, the better the engagement, right?

Well, it depends on what you mean by "better." Usually, people envision highly produced video with great motion graphics, animation, transitions, background music, professional voice-over, audio mastering, and on and on.

But, counter to what you might think, lower production value actually increases video engagement.

At first glance, this seems absurd. The less-professionally produced the product demonstration video, the more people will engage with it? That's exactly what I'm saying. Again, it's counterintuitive. But we've done our own internal tests, and the results don't lie. Here's the proof.

Testing the Lower Production Quality Theory

At Consensus, we eat, drink, and breathe demo automation, so we initially had a professionally produced video demo that incorporates a prewritten script and a voice actor. We assumed this is what our prospects wanted. But over time, customers using our software found it a difficult and lengthy process to produce video at that quality for their own demo automation.

We therefore wanted to see if applying lower production values— that is, making videos more quickly and cheaply—would get similar results. If so, we could encourage our customers to build their own demos, and they could be assured they would get good results even if the videos didn't look like they were produced by Steven Spielberg.

We were hoping we'd get at least a similar engagement rate with a lower production value. We even thought that we'd probably get a somewhat lower engagement rate given that we weren't going to put nearly the time or expense into producing the video. We weren't prepared for what we discovered.

We tested two types of demo videos, one very professionally produced and the other not. Both use the same intro video clips (those do have high production values). We wanted to test the actual demo content videos and to see how fast we could make them. So when you use the links below to compare, make sure to get past the intro video, answer the questions that will customize the demo to your preferences, and then compare the different production quality of the voice-over vs. the sales engineer.

- **Demo #1: Scripted with Professional Voice-Over** (three weeks production time)

  In the first test, we carefully scripted every word, hired a voice-over artist, and then painstakingly recorded and edited the product demo to fit the recording from the voice-over artist. It took us three weeks to complete, and that was focusing on it every day, full time, to get it just right. You can check it out here: https://www.goconsensus.com/app/view/b/958kz7v2

- **Demo #2: Non-scripted Narration by Content Expert** (three days production time)

  In the second test, we had a content expert (me to be exact) simply make an outline of what to demo, prep what to show, hit record on the screen recorder, and go to town. I spent a few hours post-editing to clean things up. Note the huge difference in production time: three days vs. three weeks. Check out the demo here: https://www.goconsensus.com/app/view/b/37kp7dfd

We were shocked at the results. The average view time in the less-produced automated demo was two minutes *longer* than the more professionally produced version. That's nearly a 300% increase in engagement. Crazy really. It took five times less time to produce (3 days instead of 15 business days), and it increased engagement threefold.

COMPARISON OF HIGH PRODUCTION VALUE
VS. AUTHENTIC DEMOS:
TABLE P : HIGH PRODUCTION VALUE

Total Views	Total Viewers	Total View Time	Average View Time
301	280	05:26:49	00:01:05

TABLE Q : AUTHENTIC SCREEN RECORDINGS

Total Views	Total Viewers	Total View Time	Average View Time
362	249	18:30:37	00:03:04

Our Customers Are Seeing a Similar Trend

Our customers are finding similar results as they experiment with lower-quality videos as well.

We were speaking with a top presales leader at Oracle recently who said, "We made a mistake early on thinking that we needed to produce the videos with high production value. We insisted on background music, a professional voice-over, cutting out any transitions in our software navigation that took too long, and so on. What we found was that the higher the production value, the more the prospect felt sold to rather than educated. We changed our approach to the concept that we wanted the viewer to feel like they were in the same room with the person doing the demo. When we did, engagement and sharing among stakeholders exploded."

Let's look at that again: "The higher the production value, the more the prospect felt sold to rather than educated."

PROSPECTS WANT TO BE EDUCATED, NOT SOLD TO

Prospects ultimately are looking for trust. They want to trust the vendor they're evaluating. They want to trust the product, and they want to trust the people backing up the product. To these viewers, high production value often screams, "We're making this glitzy because the product itself doesn't stand on its own!"

Conversely, when these viewers encounter a real sales engineer demonstrating the product in a product video, it comes across as authentic, credible, and transparent. They feel educated rather than sold to.

I think there are two main reasons why lower production values increase engagement.

Reason 1: Attitudes are shifting to transparency and openness

It used to be that higher production value caused viewers to think of the organization producing the video as more credible. The reasoning fell into two camps: "This video is poorly produced. The company producing it must not be a professional company, so it's hard to believe their product is any good" vs. "This was a very professionally produced video, so the product and interactions with this company are likely to be professional as well."

I do think some people still feel this way, but times and perceptions are changing.

According to Gartner, "The goal of TSP [Technology and Service Provider] content should be ultimately to be viewed through the lens of whether it is authentic and credible."[3]

With the rise of a generation of professionals who grew up producing and consuming video 24/7 on all kinds of devices, the younger generation has been exposed to lower-quality production videos from an early age and tend to evaluate the quality of the video more on the content than on the production quality. They're focused on questions like: "Did the video teach me something that I wanted to know? Did it bore me with irrelevant information?"

Reason 2: The YouTube Effect

Look at YouTube. Many videos with extremely low production quality get high ratings and often go viral on the merit of their content alone. While viewers today can appreciate good production quality, it isn't necessary to be considered a great video. Viewers today would much prefer video with great content over a well-produced video that doesn't have the content they want.

Look at your own behavior. How many times have you watched a video filmed by some guy behind his house showing you how to create or build something, fix something, or learn a new skill? Was it a great video? Yes—if it helped you learn what you needed. Production values were secondary to the relevance of the content to you. The same is true for the consumers of your interactive demo videos.

Think "Sales," Not "Marketing"

Before Consensus began to target sales (and specifically sales engineers) as our primary users, we had a lot of marketers who were

---

3   Gartner, *Trust Drives the B2B Technology Customer Life Cycle*, Carrie Cowan, Hank Barnes, Maria Marino, December 5, 2019.

taking the lead on demo automation inside our customer base. The marketing team would produce a set of high-level videos with great production quality, including motion graphics, voice-overs from professional artists, perfect company branding, and so on. They would build out the automated demos with this video content and then say, "Ta-da! Hey, sales team, we now have awesome automated demos for you to share with your prospects." The response from sales was underwhelming at best.

Typical responses we heard from the sales team (and still hear when marketing produces the videos) were "We can't send these out—they're just fluff and are useless" and "These won't really educate the client—they aren't what we need. We need real demos of the software."

If you're a marketer and intent on maintaining iron-fisted control over video production, get the sales team involved. Have your sales engineers and solution consultants give input on the script. Better yet, have the sales engineer record a demo and then do some post-editing.

A better practice, in my opinion, is to not involve marketing in demo video production. At Oracle, they have their sales enablement team work with sales engineers to produce the videos the sales team needs. We recommend you do the same. Don't worry about the production value. Focus on great content and engagement, and sharing will skyrocket.

CONCLUSION

Buyer enablement is the future. Buyers no longer want to engage in a lengthy process that is organized around the vendor's self-centered needs. They want to get the information they need as quickly as possible and get it out to all of the stakeholders necessary.

The challenge is that you know better what they need than they do. You're the guide through the jungle of making a complex purchase. So your job is to tell them where they are going, what pitfalls they are likely to encounter, and what resources they need to overcome and complete their journey.

Once you map out their path for them and what resources they need, it increases their confidence in you, and not only will they get there faster (which shortens your sales cycle), but it will also be a more rewarding experience, making them more likely to select you and your product as the final solution.

Feedback

I would welcome any feedback, both positive or negative, to help improve future editions of this book. What resonated with you? What didn't? If you've begun trying to implement buyer enablement, what seems to work and what doesn't?

Send me an email at garin@goconsensus.com. I'd love to chat with you.

About Consensus™

As I mentioned in the Introduction to this book, my direct experience with buyer enablement has largely been through the lens of my software company that I've built to help B2B sales teams become more successful by automating the production demonstration process using adaptive video demos.

While you can enable buying groups in a variety of ways, at Consensus we have been working on technology for several years to help make the process easier and more effective. We are best at helping midmarket and enterprise companies such as Oracle, ADP, IBM, SAP, Autodesk, Medidata, and Ivanti, usually starting with the sales and pre-sales teams, but also have small-business options.

If you would like to explore using Consensus to equip your champions with adaptive content, reach out to us by visiting goconsensus.com or sending an email to sales@goconsensus.com. You can also call us at +1 855.550.3366.

APPENDIX

To find the following samples and templates, please visit buyerenablement.io:

- Buying Group Map
- Map of Needed Information at Buying Stages
- Questions/Objections by Role
- Risks to Consider and Mitigation Strategies
- Social Proof by Stakeholder Role, Segment, Use Case
- Implementation Guide
- Buyer Enablement Sales Training Deck
- Self-Directed Automated Video Demo

ABOUT THE AUTHOR

GARIN HESS is a serial entrepreneur whose entire career has been in enterprise software, including in several roles acting as sales engineer. Garin has founded two software companies, two industry conferences, and a nonprofit organization. He is currently the founder and CEO of Consensus (goconsensus.com), the leader in intelligent demo automation software, winning the coveted Gartner recognition of "Cool Vendor." Consensus helps sales engineering teams use interactive video demos to scale productivity by reducing wasted time doing repetitive, unqualified demos so they can do more of what they do best: solutions consulting.

Outside of work, Garin enjoys reading history, mountain biking, hiking, playing tennis, community choir conducting, and spending time with his wife and their children.